Faith and Fear

DR. NORRIS D. HALL

InspiringVoices®

This book is a work of non-fiction. Unless otherwise noted, the author and the publisher make no explicit guarantees as to the accuracy of the information contained in this book and in some cases, names of people and places have been altered to protect their privacy.

Inspiring Voices books may be ordered through booksellers or by contacting:

Inspiring Voices
1663 Liberty Drive
Bloomington, IN 47403
www.inspiringvoices.com
1 (866) 697-5313

Because of the dynamic nature of the Internet, any web addresses or links contained in this book may have changed since publication and may no longer be valid. The views expressed in this work are solely those of the author and do not necessarily reflect the views of the publisher, and the publisher hereby disclaims any responsibility for them.

Any people depicted in stock imagery provided by Getty Images are models, and such images are being used for illustrative purposes only. Certain stock imagery © Getty Images.

All Scripture quotations are taken from the King James Version of the Bible.

ISBN: 978-1-4624-1279-2 (sc)
ISBN: 978-1-4624-1285-3 (hc)
ISBN: 978-1-4624-1280-8 (e)

Library of Congress Control Number: 2019911636

Print information available on the last page.

Inspiring Voices rev. date: 10/8/2019

Dedication

This book is dedicated to my husband, Alfonza, who has given me many years of love, companionship, and support. Thank you for being by my side throughout my trials and triumphs.

I also dedicate this book to the memory of my father, the late Mr. Willie D. Davis, and to my mother, the late Mrs. Alice Davis. I dedicate this book to my sisters, Eva D. Ferguson, and Linda A Wallace, to my four brothers, Pastor Bobby Davis, Melvin Davis, Willie Davis, and Carl Davis. I will always appreciate your love and support.

Introduction

The disciples were terrified after being caught in a storm. [Matthew 14:26] Jesus came to them walking on the sea. They were troubled, saying, "It is a Spirit," and they cried out for fear. They thought they were seeing a ghost. But if they had thought about all they had already seen through Jesus, they could have accepted this miracle. They were frightened, they didn't expect Jesus to come, and they weren't prepared for his help. Many times Jesus has brought us through the storms in our lives. But we still have that fear. Every time we go through the storm of life, there is fear. Faith is a mindset in which we expect God to move on our behalf. When we work upon this expectation, we can overcome our fear. No matter how adverse the conditions in your life or your mind may be, do not give up! You must remember, Jesus did not give up on you. So do not give up on Him. Trials and tribulations develop patience (Romans 5:3).

The Bible did not say we would not face trials, but when we do encounter them, the word of God will equip us to endure in all circumstances. God desires to make us complete. He will not keep us from pain, pain helps complete us, it is part of the journey. Why are you so fearful? How is it that you have no faith? The disciples lived with Jesus as a man. They did not know of Jesus as our Lord and savior. He had not died for us yet. We cannot make the same excuse. We must walk by faith and not be hindered by fear.

Contents

CHAPTER 1

Faith for the Journey

"**B**ehold, the LORD thy God hath set the land before thee: go up and possess it, as the LORD God of thy fathers hath said unto thee; neither be discouraged [Deuteronomy 1:22]."

God gave the land to His people and told them to take possession of it. By remaining outside the land, the Israelites were disobeying God. When God offers a gift, He provides it in good faith. However, when He opens opportunities, we have doubts and are afraid of failure. Seize your opportunities to grow, to share your faith, and to live in a manner pleasing to God. He will lead the way and give you strength.

FAITH is the substance of things hoped for, the evidence of things not seen [Hebrews 11:1] two words describes our faith: confidence and certainty. These two qualities need a secure beginning and ending point. The beginning point of faith is the belief in God's character He is who He says He is. The point is the belief in God's promises. He will do what He says He will do. We believe that God will fulfill his obligations even though we don't see those promises materializing. This is when we demonstrate true faith.

The disciples were given the authority to do the healing, but they had not yet learned how to appropriate the power of God. Jesus' frustration is with the unbelieving and unresponsive generation. His disciples were merely a reflection of that attitude, in this instance. Jesus's purpose was not to criticize the disciples but to encourage them to greater faith. The disciples had been unable to cast out this Devil, and they asked Jesus why? He pointed to their lack of confidence. It is the power of God, plus our faith, that moves mountains. The mustard seed was the smallest particle. Jesus said that even faith as small or undeveloped as a mustard seed would have been sufficient. Some we try to move on our power, with our own ability rather than God's. There is excellent potential in even a little faith when we trust in God's power to act. If we feel weak or powerless as Christians. We should examine our faith, making sure we are trusting God's power, not our abilities to produce results. And Jesus said unto them, "Because of your unbelief: for verily I say unto you If you have faith as a grain of mustard seed, ye shall say the mountain, move hence to yonder place, and it shall remove: and nothing shall be impossible unto you." (Matthew 17:20, Jesus wasn't condemning the disciples for substandard faith; he was trying to show how important principle would be in their future ministry. If you are facing a problem that seems as big and immovable as a mountain, turn your eyes from the mountain and look to Christ for deeper faith. Only then will you be able to overcome the obstacles that stand in your way. What Jesus is teaching is that some work for God is more complicated and requires more than the usual dependence on God. This verse does not mean that prayer and fasting alone would have accomplished the miracle. Prayer and fasting indicate faith, discipline, and humility before God, without which there can be no hope of success. Those who Seek God believe in His goodness, obey His commands, regulate their life on the promises of God. They refuse the pleasures of sin, endure persecution, perform mighty acts of righteousness, and suffer for God. Faith is being obedient to your God whom you have never seen.

Without faith, it is impossible to please Him (Jesus Christ) for he that cometh to God must believe that He is and that He is a reward for them that diligently seek Him [Hebrews 11:6]. Understanding that God exists is only the beginning; even the demons believe that much. God wants your faith to lead to a dynamic personal relationship.

For example, Abraham, when he was called to go out into a foreign land. It was his faith that made Abraham want to obey. He left his own country without knowing where he was going. With faith, he lived as a foreigner in that country as did Isaac and Jacob, who received the same promise from God. That they would inherit it. [Hebrew 11:9].

If God commands you to do something out of the ordinary, by faith do it. [Matthew 17:20] because of your unbelief, for verily, I say unto you. If you have faith as a grain of mustard seed, ye shall say unto this mountain, remove hence to yonder place, and it shall remove, and nothing shall be impossible unto you.

Jesus was not condemning the disciples for substandard faith. He was trying to show how important the principle would be in their ministry. If you are facing a problem that seems big and immovable as a mountain, turn your eyes from the mountain and look to Christ for deeper faith.

FEAR wants you to feel like you are in danger all the time, it wants you to feel pain, and trouble is surrounding you. Fear is being worried. It will make you uneasy, and the devil will bring fear to you if you listen.

Paul said to Timothy in [2 Timothy 1:17] For God hath not given us the spirit of fear, but of power and of love, and of a sound mind. I urged you to be bold. Do not let people intimidate you.

The power of the Holy Spirit can help you overcome your fear.

It would be wonderful if God just laid out the whole picture of our life and said, here is where you are going, here is everything that is going to happen before you get there. Here is each day of your life for the next 20 years, and here is how it is going to turn out. That is destiny. If He did that, our lives would not require faith. God is not going to lay everything out for you; He will give you one piece of the puzzle at a time. Each piece connected to the other part will create a perfect picture of God's plan for life, but those pieces must be held together by faith in His word. Every step you take must be a step of faith.

[Psalm 37:23] says, the steps of a good man are ordered by the Lord. God, right now, is building something in your life. Refuse to fear anything that would stand in your way; there is no failure in God.

The Bible teaches that without faith, it is impossible to please God. Let your dreams be fulfilled by faith. The thing many people fear in life is a failure. They fear that if they step out in their goals, everything will fall apart. This is fear.

Jesus said, "if you draw nigh unto me, I will draw nigh unto you." We cannot set there waiting for Jesus to do it all for us. [Revelation 3:20] behold, I stand at the door and knock if any man hears my voice, and open the door, I will come into him, and will sup with him, and he with me.

The Laodicean church was complacent and wealthy. They felt self-satisfied, but they did not have Christ's presence among them. He knocked at the door of their hearts, but they were so busy enjoying worldly pleasures that they did not notice that He was trying to enter. The pleasures of this world. Money, security, and material possessions are dangerous. Their temporary satisfaction makes us indifferent to God's offer of lasting happiness. If you find yourself feeling indifferent to church, to God, or to the Bible, you may have begun to shut God out of your life. Leave the door of your heart always open to God, and you will not need to worry about missing his knock. Letting Him in is your only hope for lasting fulfillment.

Jesus is knocking on the door of our hearts. Every time we sense it, we should turn to Him. He wants to have fellowship with us, and He wants us open to Him. He is patient and persistent in trying to get through to us, not breaking and entering, but knocking. He allows us to decide whether or not to open our lives to Him. Do you intentionally keep his life-changing presence and power on the other side of the door?

[Micah 7:7-8] "Therefore, I will look unto the LORD; I will wait for the God of my salvation: my God will hear me." "Rejoice not against me, O mine enemy: when I fall, I shall arise; when I sit in darkness, the LORD shall be a light unto me."

Micah showed great faith in God when he proclaimed that he would wait upon God. God hears and saves when help is needed. God would bring him through when times were tough. He would be patient because God would bring him out of the darkness. We, too, can have a relationship with God that can allow us to have confidence like Micah's. It does not take unusual talent; it simply takes faith in God and willingness to act on the faith. When I fall, "I shall arise." Not if I fall, but when I fall.

I will look unto the Lord; I will wait for the God of my salvation. My God will hear me. That is how God wants His children to speak. God always rejoices when we stand on faith. Satan is the one who plots against you, especially when you make mistakes. Satan is the one who brings you doubt. He tries to get you to wallow in self-doubt, feel sorry for yourself. Satan will talk to you if you let him. Satan will tell you that you will never have anything, that you will never make it in life.

Every time you make a mistake, Satan rejoices. No one is without mistakes, we have all stumbled, and we have all fallen at some time or another. We do not plan to fall sometimes we do. So we fall down, but we get up and ask for God's forgiveness and go on with your life, In fact, we will probably make a few more mistakes along the way. My brothers and sisters, it's not a failure to fall, it is only a failure to stay down when you do fall.

Micah said that when I fall, I shall arise. There will be a place and a time in your life when you finally decide once and for all that when I fall, I will rise again no matter how far I have fallen. When you fall the devil expects you to quit, he wants you to say, where is God? He wants you to get discouraged and be fearful.

The devil wants to stop you from stepping out into the biggest dreams and desires of your life. He wants you to be afraid of everything. These are Gods rewards to us. These are the promises that drive our will that when you fall, it is not over. God wants you to be determined that no matter how many times you fall, with the support of His hand, you shall arise.

[John 10:10] tells you the thief cometh not, but for to steal and to kill and to destroy. But Jesus said I come that they might have life and that they might have it more abundantly. God wants you to live the abundant life, walk in prosperity, and live in His absolute best at all times.

Does it seem that some believers walk in abundance, while others never seem to? There is a God who promises to bring us wealth. But there is also a thief who wants to steal, kill, and destroy everything that God has promised us. Satan's goal is to take your dreams because he knows that if he can do that he can ruin your future. If you feed your fears, your faith will starve. Feed your faith, starve your fears.

Satan wants you to have money. He wants you covered in jewelry. He wants to go after your car or your house. His desire is something far more precious. He wants your peace of mind and your joy. As he takes your worldly possessions, he breaks down your faith. His name is Fear. His task is to break your courage and leave you timid and trembling. His mission is to manipulate you with mysteries, to taunt you with the unknown. Fear of death, failure, of God, and of tomorrow-his arsenal is vast. His goal is to create cowardly, joyless souls.

[Lamentations 3:57] You drew near on the day I called on you, and said, "Do not fear!" Amidst the olive trees [Gethsemane's garden,] Jesus "fell to the ground. He prayed that, if it were possible, the awful hour awaiting him might pass him by. 'Abba, Father,' he cried out, 'everything is possible for you. Please take this cup of suffering away from me. Yet I want your will to be done, not mine.'

The cup equaled Jesus' worst-case scenario: to be the recipient of Gods wrath. He had never felt God's fury: he did not deserve to. He had never experienced isolation from His Father: the two had been one for eternity. He had never known physical death; He was an immortal being. Yet within a few short hours, Jesus would face them all. And Jesus was afraid. Deathly afraid, and what He did with His fear shows us what to do with ours

He prayed Jesus faced His ultimate fear with honest prayer. We need to hear that God is still in control. We need to understand that it is not over until He says so. We need to hear that life's mishaps and tragedies are not a reason to bail out. They are simply a reason to sit tight.

When the train goes through a tunnel and the world gets dark, do you jump out? No! You sit still and trust the engineer to get you through." Next time you are disappointed, do not panic. Do not jump out. Do not give up. Just be patient and let God remind you He is still in control.

Do not let Satan steal your dreams. He cannot have your future; it is up to you to stop him. You are a threat to him as long as you continue to pursue all that God has for you. Walk in your abundance that God has promised you. Do not let the devil steal your joy!

[Acts 10:38] Jesus heals all who were oppressed by the devil. If Satan is challenging and suppressing you, it does not mean defeat. It could be a clear sign that you are doing something that is making him afraid.

Satan is the father of all lies. That means everything he says to you is a lie. He tells you that you deserve a financial breakthrough in your life, and it is a lie. Hope is one thing, but God decides our just deserts. When he tells you that you will never be healed, it is a lie. When he tells you that you will never fulfill your dreams, it is a lie.

The Bible says that God cannot lie. If God says that you are healed, you are healed. If God says that you are to live an abundant life, then it is so. If God has told you that He is able to do exceedingly, abundantly above all that you can ever ask or think, then it is so.

Many believers quickly acknowledge that the devil is a liar but forget that everything God says is right. When you believe what God says, there is no need to be afraid of what the devil says.

Fear is not a product of anything God says. The product of God's Word is faith [Romans 10:17] tells us, so then faith cometh by hearing, and hearing by the Word of God. When we consistently listen to the Word of God, faith is produced. On the other hand, when we listen to the voice of the devil, fear is generated. Three words should never come out of the mouth of the believer, I am afraid. The devil hears when you say that you are scared he immediately goes to work on your mind.

[Proverbs 18:21] says, the power of life and death is in the tongue. If you speak, I am afraid, that is what the devil wants you to say when you are under pressure, and it looks as if everything you are going through is impossible to overcome. The devil loves it when Christians start to question God. The strongest way you can question God's integrity is to say that you are afraid. When the devil tells you there is no way out of your situation, it is a lie when he tells you God is not hearing your prayer, it is a lie.

The devil may try to tell you that your children will never get saved. He may say that he is going to destroy your marriage. According to [Hebrews 11:1], faith is the substance of things hoped for. Fear is the substance of things dreaded.

It is important to remember that when God speaks, faith comes. On the other hand, when Satan speaks fear comes if you listen. Too many people lean on what the devil says and end up being controlled by fear. If we lean on what God says, it brings faith and gives us the ability to conquer everything that comes our way.

I encourage you to consume your life with the Word of God.

Do not do it as a religious duty but as a faith developing tool to help you achieve your dreams.

Spend time in the presence of God. If you spend time with God, fear will be replaced by faith. Right now, you might feel as if you are at the bottom of the barrel. You may feel as if everything you have done has amounted to nothing. You may have been told that you have fallen too far down to get back up. Now is the time to look to the Word and declare: When I fall, I shall arise. I do not care how far down you are. You can rise, get back up, and allow God to help you recognize his gifts are more than this moment. Get up, clean yourself off, and give God the glory.

CHAPTER 2

It's Time to Recapture Your Dreams

"Repent ye therefore, and be converted, that your sins may be blotted out when the times of refreshing shall come from the presence of the Lord." And he shall send Jesus Christ, which before was preached unto you: Whom the heaven must receive until the times of restitution of all things, which God hath spoken by the mouth of all his holy prophets since the world began [Acts 3:19-21].

God has chosen to bless His people with the outpouring of the Holy Spirit only on the conditions of repentance, turning from sin and the unrighteous ways of their surrounding perverse generation, and conversion, turning to God, listening to everything that Christ, the prophet, tells them, and ever moving toward sincere obedience to Christ.

Throughout this present age and until the return of Christ, God will send "times of refreshing" (the outpouring of the Holy Spirit) to all who repent and are converted. Although perilous times will come toward the end of this age and a great falling away from the faith will occur, God still promises to send revival and times of refreshing upon the faithful. The presence of Christ, spiritual blessings, miracles, and outpourings of the Holy Spirit will come upon the remnant that faithfully seeks Him and overcome the world, the flesh, and the dominion of Satan.

"The times of restitution of all things" refers to the time of Christ's return from heaven to put down evil and establish the kingdom of God on earth free from all sin. Christ will redeem or renovate all nature and reign personally on the earth. Note that not people on earth, but Christ and the armies from heaven will bring in the triumph of God and His kingdom.

It's Time to Recapture Your Dreams. God is ready to restore something in your life, He wants to restore everything that Satan has stolen from you, including your dreams. If you are not winning yet, don't give up. God is not through with your song, please be patient with me God is not through with me.

If you've made mistakes and had setbacks, just remember that God is the God of restoration. It is time to take back what the Devil has tried to take away from you. The Devil thinks that he can take away what God has promised you, he does not have the authority to do so. God has given you the power to possess what is yours, so don't give up.

Every dream that God drops in your heart begins with a picture of that dream before it becomes a reality. You have to see it on the inside of you when you study the Bible, and you discover a promise from God. That promise is designed by the Holy Spirit to be painted on the inside of you.

3 John 1:2 "Beloved, I wish above all things that thou mayest prosper and be in health." It is normally God's will that believers be healthy and that our lives be accompanied by His blessings. He wants us to prosper that our work, plans, purposes, ministry, families go according to God's will and direction. God's blessings that come to us through the redemption of Christ include both physical and spiritual needs.

Proverbs 23:7 Tells us for as he thinketh in his heart, so is he. Acts 26:16 Jesus said to Paul but rise, and stand upon thy feet: for I have appeared unto thee for this purpose, to make the minister Jesus told Paul that he had appeared to him for a particular purpose Jesus had a special purpose for Paul. This same Jesus has a special meaning for your life and mine He talks to us through His Word by His Spirit. He speaks to give a purpose. This is while it is important to spend time with Jesus. He has a purpose for each one of us, the only way to know that purpose is to spend time with Him. You will see as you fellowship with Him, you will begin to have a clear understanding of what He wants you to do with your life. Have you ever seen people who seem to have no goals, no dreams, no vision, no purpose? These are not the kind of people you want to keep company with. If you're not watchful, these people will pull you away from your dream. They will hinder you from fulfilling your purpose.

Paul, a servant of Jesus Christ, called to be an apostle said, "if thou shall confess with thy mouth the Lord Jesus and shalt believe in thine heart that God hath raised him from the dead thou shalt be saved [Romans 10:9]." Salvation is as close as your own mouth and heart. People think it must be a complicated process, but it is not. If we believe in our hearts and say with our mouths that Christ is the risen Lord, we will be saved. Don't share impossible things with those people who do not believe that all things are possible to those who believe. You can confess with your mouth, but it must get in the heart.

Proverbs 13:20 tells us that He that walketh with wise men shall be wise: but a companion of fools shall be destroyed. When most people need advice, they go to their friends first, because friends accept them and usually agree with them. But that is why they may not be able to help them with difficult problems. Our friends are so much like us that they may not have any answers we haven't already heard. Instead, we should seek out older and wiser people to advise us. Knowledgeable people have experienced a lot in life and have succeeded, they are not afraid, to tell the truth. Who are the wise, godly people who can warn you of the pitfalls ahead? So many people are destroyed for lack of knowledge [Hosea 4:6]. Why are they destroyed? Because they have rejected knowledge and forgotten the law of your God.

We need to be stirred up and encouraged every now and then, we need an atmosphere of faith. Not of doubt and fear. Many time people let go of their dreams and what God has called them to do, because of what people say. We have to walk by faith, not by sight. Always remember when God gives you a dream He will take you through it, it might not be easy. But our responsibility is to hold on to it no matter how impossible it may appear to be.

Problems occur in every area of life. The Christians life may have more stormy weather than calm seas. As Christ's followers, be prepared for the storms that will surely come. Do not surrender to stress but remain resilient and recover from setbacks. With faith in Christ, you can pray, trust, and move ahead. When a storm approaches, lean into the wind and trust God. We so many times are just like the disciples, they lived with Jesus, but they underestimated him. They did not see that his power applied to their own situation. The disciples did not yet know enough about Jesus. We cannot make the same excuse. Many have wondered about Jesus' statement that if we have faith and don't doubt, we can move mountains. Jesus, of course, was suggesting that his followers use prayer as "magic" and perform capricious mountain-moving acts. Instead, he was making a strong point about the disciples' (and our) lack of faith. What kinds of mountains do you face? Have you talked to God about them? How secure is your faith?

It is time for you to claim your dreams, your gifts, do not let the devil take it away from you. People may even criticize you when you have goals. When you have a dream, do not look for a man to praise you. All your help comes from the Lord.

Moses had a dream and the courage to do what God had told him to do. God sent Moses and Aaron to tell Pharaoh "Thus saith the Lord, God of Israel, let my people go, . . ." that they may hold a feast unto me in the wilderness. God spoke to Moses from an unexpected source: a burning bush. When Moses saw it, he went to investigate. God often uses unexpected sources when working in our lives, whether people, thoughts, or experiences. Be willing to examine and be open to God's surprise.

And afterward, Moses and Aaron went in, and told Pharaoh, Thus saith the Lord God of Israel, Let my people go, that they may hold a feast unto me in the wilderness. And Pharaoh said, who is the LORD, that I should obey his voice to let Israel go? I know not the Lord, neither will I let Israel go. And they said, The God of the Hebrews hath met with us: let us go, we pray thee, three days' journey into the desert, and sacrifice unto the LORD our God; lest he falls upon us with pestilence, or with the sword {Exodus 4:1-3}.

Pharaoh would not listen to Moses and Aaron because he did not know or respect God. People who do not know God may not listen to his Word or his messengers. Like Moses and Aaron, we need to persist. When others reject you or your faith, don't be surprised or discouraged. Continue to tell them about God, trusting him to open minds and soften stubborn hearts.

Moses and Aaron took their message to Pharaoh just as God directed. The unhappy result was harder work and more oppression for the Hebrews. Sometimes hardship comes as a result of obeying God. Are you following God but still suffering –or suffering even worse than before? If your life is miserable, don't assume you have fallen out of God's favor. You may be suffering for doing good in an evil world.

Moses is no longer fearful. He's not afraid to step out in faith, this is not the same man. The old Moses had all kinds of excuses, this man is now boldly demanding that Pharaoh let God's people go. Moses now had what I like to call a no-quit attitude, he will not give up until his dream had become a reality. God is looking for believers who are not afraid or fearful. He is looking for people who are willing to talk more about what God can do than about what He cannot do, we can do all things through Christ Jesus.

Walk by faith and do not fear, are you willing to walk out on faith? It's time for you to recapture your dreams. If God tells you that your dreams will come true, if God tells you that He can do exceedingly, abundantly above all that you can ever all or think. God will do for us not only more than we ask and desire in prayer but also even more than our imagination can perceive. This promise is conditioned and dependent upon the degree of the Holy Spirit's presence, power, and grace operating in our life. Now unto him, that can do exceeding abundantly above all that we ask or think, according to the power that worketh in us {Ephesians 3:20}.

God doesn't always work in the way that seems best to us, if God does not lead you along the shortest path to your dream, don't complain or resist follow him, trust Him to lead you safely around unseen obstacles. God can see the end of your journey from the beginning, and He knows the safest and best route.

And when Pharaoh drew nigh, the children of Israel lifted up their eyes, and, behold, the Egyptians marched after them; and they were sore afraid: and the children of cried out unto the Lord. And they said unto Moses because there were no graves in Egypt, hast thou has taken us away to die in the wilderness? Wherefore hast thou dealt thus with us, to carry us forth out of Egypt (Exodus 14:10-11)?

Trapped against the sea, the Israelites faced the Egyptian army sweeping in for the kill. The Israelites thought they were doomed. After watching God's mighty hand deliver them from Egypt, their only response was fear, whining, and despair. Where was their trust in God? Israel had to learn from repeated experience that God was able to provide for them. God has preserved these examples in the Bible so that we can learn to trust him the first time. By focusing on God's faithfulness in the past, we can face crises with confidence rather than with fear and complaining.

This is the first instance of grumbling and complaining by the Israelites. Grumbling would become a major problem for the people on this journey. Yet how often do we find ourselves doing the same thing complaining over inconveniences or discomfort? The Israelites were about to learn some tough lessons. Had they trusted God, they would have been spared much grief.

The people were hostile and despairing, but Moses encouraged then to watch the wonderful way God would rescue them. Moses had a positive attitude! When it looked as if they were trapped, he called upon God to intervene. We may not be chased by an army, but we may still feel trapped. Instead of giving in to despair, we should adopt Moses attitude to "stand still, and see the salvation of the LORD."

Faith is not the product of reason; it is the product of the reborn human spirit. It is not the product of the mind but the product of the heart. Faith is a powerful force. It is a physical force. It is a conductive force. It will move things. Faith will change things. Faith will change the human body. It will change the human mind. It will break the human heart. Faith will change circumstances.

Let's look at fear, the negative side of the coin. Fear is not a mental force. Fear is a spiritual force, and I will tell you where it came from.

God created a man called Adam, and He gave this man faith. Adman was called the son of God because he was born of God. God created his physical body from the dust of the earth, but the agency had no life in it. It was just meat and bones. Then God breathed into Adam the breath or spirit of life. God's spirit was breathed into Adam. He was a magnificent, powerful creature. With his faith, he had dominion over the forces of nature. He had control over everything that walked, crawled, swam, and moved. This same man committed high treason, bowed his knee to a spiritual outlaw, and gave unto him his authority to rule the earth. Adam gave the broad power that God had given him into the hands of Satan, and when he did, spiritual death moved into his spirit. The life of God departed, and the presence of his new god overcame him. Everything about him was perverted. The faith force that was born into Adam when God breathed His life into him was perverted and turned into the force that we know and recognize as fear. Fear ruled Adam from that moment. And the first words from his mouth were, I was afraid.

Fear activates Satan the way faith activates God. Why does the world not accept the logic that if fear, a spiritual force, will make a man sick then faith, the opposite spiritual force, will make him well? If the power will make him well. If the force of fear can imprison a man or woman, then the strength of faith can make him free. Why do men and women have confidence in fear and not in faith? They are reasoning outside the Word of God. They are reasoning inside the world's order. On the other hand, we are reasoning in the world of the spirit by the Word of God.

"For by grace are ye saved through faith; and that not of yourself: it is the gift of God" (Ephesians 2:8). Everything in this verse is the gift of God. Grace is the gift of God. The salvation is the gift of God, and the faith to receive salvation is the gift of God. This faith is the gift of God: it is not of yourself. The faith that was imparted to you is God's own brand of faith.

CHAPTER 3

Patient

Do you ever get down in the dumps you feel that everything you have dreamed about, everything you have waited for everything you planned for, everything you lived for just going down the drain because of the enemy you wonder when the storm will end, you are just tired, of being tired?

Sometimes seem like you just want to throw up your hands and just quit. How many know that God does not come in every storm? He is teaching patients and how to wait, how to stand, have faith, and wait on Him.

David said For His anger is but for a moment, His favor is for life. Weeping may endure for a night, but joy comes in the morning. Jesus desires to perfect the woman's faith and to lead her to a public confession of faith. He rewards her testimony with the assurance that she can go in peace. I know when we are going through the storm of life, our faith is weak.

(Mark 4:40) Jesus asks the question, "why are you so fearful how is it that you have no hope?" They lived with Jesus, but they underestimated his ability. They did not see that his power applied to their own situation. Jesus had been with his people for 20 centuries, and yet we are like the disciples underestimate his ability to handle any crises in our lives. The disciples did not yet know enough about Jesus. We are his children, and we cannot make the same excuse, we all have some issues we need the Lord to help us with.

You don't learn Faith when you have a lot of money, you learn FAITH when your money runs short. When you need to pay a bill and don't have any money. You don't learn FAITH when you are feeling good in the body, you learn FAITH when pains are raking through your body. When you can say though he slays me yet, I will trust him.

It is FAITH when you go to God for something, and you know it is going to be granted to you just go on and say Amen it is done. The power of God isn't activated by just the incidental touch I am sure that day a lot of people reached through the crowd and touched Jesus out of curiosity to see if anything would happen, the power of God isn't activated by the curious touch you have got to stir up your faith. Before you reach out for Jesus, you had better stir up your faith, God moves by FAITH not by curiosity.

Somebody may be saying right now I have been through so much. I feel so broken I just need a miracle in my life. The miracles are coming out of the broken pieces of your life. So many times, when we are going through the storm, we have to wait on the Lord. Sometimes you have to mix FAITH and patience together and wait on the Lord.

Stop sitting around, feeling sorry for yourself, waiting on someone to pat you on the back. When we are going through, we want someone to help carry our weight someone to help us bear our pains. The only man I know who can carry our burdens is Jesus.

Stop feeling sorry for yourself. Jesus said that if you abide in me and my words abide in you, you will ask what you will and it shall be done for you. There is greatness on the inside of you stop sitting around waiting on someone to encourage you Greater is he that lives in you than he that lives in the world.

You cannot hurry God, you have got to be patient with him to act on your behalf. In this life, you will experience troubles and hardships. But when you think of all His goodness and all he has done for you, Give him glory and praise him. If you are waiting until the sun shines in your life, if you are waiting for every day to be sunny before you give him though, you might not never thank him.

There will be storms in our life; sometimes God will move that storm, sometimes he will ride the storm out with you. (Genesis 6:3), And the LORD said. My spirit shall not always strive with man, for that he also as flesh yet his days shall be a hundred and twenty years. What patience God showed, allowing the people of Noah's day 120 years to change their sinful ways, God shows his great patience with us as well. He is giving time to stop living our way and begin living, the way he shows us in his Word. While 120 years seems like a long time, eventually time ran out, and the floodwaters swept across the earth. Your time also may be running out. Turn to God to forgive your sins.

Noah occasionally sent a bird out to test the earth and see if it was dry, but he didn't get out of the ark until God told him to. He was waiting for God's timing. God knew that even though the water was gone, the earth was not dry enough for Noah and his family to venture out. What patience Noah, especially after spending an entire year inside his boat WE, like Noah, must trust God to give us patience those difficult times when we wait

(Thessalonians 1:4) So that we glory in you in the churches of God for your patience and faith in all your persecutions and tribulations that ye endure. As a believer, you are not left to your own resources to cope with problems, Even when you don't know the right words to pray, the Holy Spirit prays with and for you, and God answers. With GOD helping you pray, you don't need to be afraid to come before him. Ask the Holy Spirit to lead you 'according to the will of God.' Then when you bring your requests to God, trust that he will always do what is best. He may not answer you prays at that hour, be patience to wait on him; he knows what we need better than we do. (Psalm 74:1) O God, why hast thou cast us off forever? Why doth thine anger smoke against the sheep of thy pasture God's hot anger against Israel had grown during the many years of their sin and idolatry. His patience endured for generations, but at last, it was set aside for judgment. If you fall into sin and quickly seek God's forgiveness, his mercy may come soon, and his anger may leave quickly. But if you practice sin against him for a long time, don't be surprised if his patience runs out. The father watched and waited. He was dealing with a human being with a will if his own, but he was ready to greet his son if he returned.

In the same way, God's love is constant and waiting. He will search for us and give us opportunities to respond, but he does not force us to come to him. Like the father, he waits patiently for us to come to our senses.

The keys to surviving suffering and persecution are patience and faith. When faced with crushing troubles and hardships, we and difficulties, we can have confidence that God is using them for our good and for his glory. Knowing that God is fair and just gives us patience in our suffering because we know that he has not forgotten us, in his timing, he will relieve our pain and punish those who persecute us. Do you trust God's timing? That is the first step toward growing in endurance and faithfulness.

As we live for Christ, we will experience troubles and hardships because we are trying to be God's people in a perverse world. Some people say that crises are the result are sin or lack of faith, but Paul teaches that they may be a part of God's plan for believers. Our problems can help us look upward and forward. Your troubles may be an indication that you are taking a stand for Christ. When you do so, you are experiencing the privilege of showing that you are worthy of God's Kingdom.

Don't give up have patience, wait on the Lord, while you are waiting on the Lord the Devil will try your FAITH. You have got to remind that Devil that you have authority over him. Remind the Devil that there is nothing he can do to stop you. Remind

Satan that the Lord is a light unto you and your destiny is in God's hands. Remind Satan that God is always with you when I'm up, and when I'm down when I'm going through my trials, He is there.

Even the strongest people get tired at times, but God is always there to renew your strength. He is never too tired or too busy to help or listen. When you feel all life crushing you and cannot go another step, you can always call upon Jesus to renew your strength. Just be Patient when he asks you to wait. It is human nature to make our own plans, and then ask God to bless them. We should seek God's will; first, God might have another plan for our lives by communicating with him. We allow him to counsel us and give us wisdom.

You have been blessed for success God has healing with your name on it. New dreams with your name on it. Because he finds favor in you. It's not what you want for your life; it's what God wants for you when God says NO, don't worry because He sees your Past He knows what's in it. And He knows what your future hold.

Waiting on GOD is not easy, often it seems that he isn't answering our prayers, or doesn't understand the urgency of our situation. God is worth waiting for. If we wait, prayers will be answered. God wants to carry our burdens. But often we try to take them ourselves even when we say we are trusting him.

Have you ever felt as if you have hit rock bottom, everything is going wrong and getting worse, no matter how you feel tell it to God? The high and Holy God came down to our level to save us because it is impossible for us to go up to his level to protect ourselves. We have got to thank God, not for our problems, but for the strength, he is building in you through the difficulties of life, if you just hold on, God will see you through.

When you hold on in this life, you will learn that God is our high and mighty refuge, and he is our provider. You may have been told that you do not have to remind God of anything, He already knows everything. "That is so true" But in (Isaiah 43:26) God said put me in remembrance, God Invites us to remind him of His Word. When we remind God of His Word, we are just calling His attention to what he already promised us.

Ask God for what you want, but don't be surprised when he gives you what you really need. (Philippians 4:19). But my God shall supply all your need according to his riches in glory by Jesus. We can be sure and trust that God will always meet our needs, Not our wants. Whatever we need on the earth, God will always supply. Many times we have to have patience and wait on Him, patience is a part of our walk with God. So when uncertainty arises, we pray, have faith be patience and wait on God. Our goal is to know Jesus Christ, to be like Him, to be all Jesus had in mind for us. We should not let anything take our eyes off our goal, which is Jesus Christ. (Psalm 37:7) Rest in the LORD. And wait patiently for him: fret not thyself because of him who prospereth in his way; because of the man who bringeth wicked devices to pass. To commit ourselves to the Lord means to trust him, believing that he can care for us better than we care for ourselves.

If you are carrying your past along with you every day, leave that past alone, you can not go back and fix not one thing. That pass made you realized that you need Jesus, it's time to grow up in the knowledge of God. If you ask Jesus will forgive you, move on to a life of Faith and obedience.

It means building the will to say no when a powerful appetite inside you are screaming yes. Train yourself diligently because your spiritual progress depends upon it. Tell God about it every morning when he wakes you up, just tell him, Lord, this is another day that you have made. Just tell him, Lord, I thank you for open my eyes to see another day that you made. Thank you for bringing us over from day to day didn't have to do it, but you did.

CHAPTER 4

Faith and Fear

To fear the LORD is to recognize him for who he is: holy, almighty, pure, all-knowing, all-powerful, all-wise. When we see God in this light, we also see ourselves for who we are: sinful, weak, frail (Mark 6:49-50). The disciples were afraid, but Jesus' presence calmed their fears when you experience fear, do you try to deal with it yourself, or do you let Jesus deal with it? In times of fear and uncertainty, it is calming to know that Christ is always with you. To recognize his presence is the antidote for fear.

We don't know how to deal with storms, we are like the disciples we get afraid. God tells you to fear not for I am with you. Be not dismayed for I am your God, I will strengthen you I will help you. I will uphold you with my righteous right hand. In the storm of life, we always say, I got it, I got it under control. Jesus is challenging you to rise to a new level, another level so that you will be able to see what his power is all about.

[Matthew 14:28-29}. And Peter answered him and said LORD if it is thou, bid me come unto thee on the water. VS. 29, and he said come, and when Peter was come down out of the ship, he walked on water to go to Jesus. We never know what kind of storm we will meet in this life. The storm life comes in so many ways, so many times when we are not looking. When we are thinking that everything is fine and up pop a storm. Many times we try to take the storm in our hands. The storms of life are no match for you and me, we can't weather the storm. There is a Wonderful old hymn which says – he gives us peace in the midst of the storm. We don't know how to deal with the storm, we are like the disciples we get afraid.

The only authority that they have over this storm is a voice of fear. The devil smells fear when He can find a little fear, He will come in and work with your mind He will wear you out. We have to remember that God has given to us Power, Love, and a Sound mind. Let me help somebody right now. You got to watch out for fear. The disciples were in the middle of a storm, the only thing they could think: If Jesus were here

He would handle this storm. They were out on the sea, and the ship looked like it was going to turn over. They had seen Jesus handle a storm and needed to handle this one.

He has brought them through one storm. But Jesus said to them: O ye of little faith. What I am saying if Jesus brought you through a storm last year, He would bring you through this year. There were three words said: Peace Be Still; and the storm ceased.

We may not walk on water, but we do walk through tough situations, keep your eyes on Jesus He will bring you through the storm of life. God knows when his children need help, He knows when the load gets too heavy. God knows when the road gets rough. Just remember God will show up when you are in your storm, He will show up when you think you just can't take no more. Jesus will show up to wipe your tears away. He will show up to let you know you are not alone.

You wonder when will the storm end. You are just tired of being tired. Sometimes seem like you just want to throw up your hands and quit. Keep the faith because God does not come in every storm. He is teaching you patience, and how to wait, and have faith. I know when you are going through the storm of life, our faith gets a little weak.

[Mark 4:40], Jesus asked the question why are you so fearful? How is it that you have no faith? The disciples lived with Jesus, but they underestimated him. They did not see that his power applied to their own situation. The disciples did not yet know enough about Jesus. So many times, when we are going through the storm of life, we have to wait on the Lord, sometimes we have to mix faith and patient together and wait.

Sometime when you pray to Him, He will calm your storm, and someday, He will step on board and ride the storm out with you. Sometimes you have to press your way, but don't give up. If God didn't give you no rough roads to walk, if he didn't give us no mountains to climb, if He didn't give you no battles to fight, we wouldn't grow. Sometimes it takes trials and tribulations to keep us humble, sometimes it takes tests to keep us on our knees. I know the sun does not shine every day in your life but thank God for saving you.

I am so glad we don't have to walk this road by ourselves, I am happy that we have a Comforter, not only a Comforter, but we have a Strengthener, Counselor, Helper, Adviser, Advocate and a Friend that will stick closer than a brother, we have Jesus. Just trust Him to lead you safely through your storm of life, around your unseen obstacles. He sees the end of your journey from the beginning, and He knows the safest and best way to leaves. Sometimes He will lead us through the valley and sometime He will carry us to the mountain top.

Wait on the Lord, I don't know what kind of storm you are going through, have faith don't fear, you may have to wait some time with tears in your eye but wait. God come on his on time, not your time.

We may not walk on water, but we do walk through tough situations. If we take our eyes off Jesus, we will sink. Keep your eyes on Jesus He will bring you through the storm. God knows when his children need help, He knows when the load gets heavy. He knows when the road gets rough. He sees us day after day toiling in rowing. He will show up when you think you can't take any more. He will show up to let you know that you are not alone. Just say I can do all things through Christ Jesus who strengthens me. Don't make the mistake that Peter made don't look at the tough situation, step out on FAITH.

God will show up in your storm when you think you just can't take more, He will show up and wipe your tears away. He will show up to let you know you are not alone. Come out the dump, stop feeling that everything you have dreamed about, everything you have waited for, everything you have planned for, everything you are living for, just gone down the drain because of the enemy. You wonder when will the storm end. You are just tired of being tied some time you wish to throw up your hands and quit. Have faith God does not come in every storm some time He will step on board and ride the storm out with you.

God teacher you faith and patient, not fear. When we are going through the storm of life, our faith gets weak.

Mark 4:40, Jesus asked the question. Why are you so fearful, how is it that you have no faith? The disciples lived with Jesus, but in the storm, they were so afraid. They did not see that his power applied to their own situation.

Jesus had been with his people for twenty centuries and yet like the disciples underestimate His power to handle crises in our lives. The disciples did not yet know enough about Jesus. We cannot make the same excuse. The power of God isn't activated by the curious touch you have got to stir up your faith. Before you reach out for Jesus, you had better stir up your faith. God moves by faith, not curious.

I have been through so much, I feel so broken I just need a miracle in my life. The miracles are coming out of the broken pieces of my life. So many times, when we are going through the storm of experience, we have to have faith trust God He won't let you down.

Sometimes you have to mix faith and patents together and

wait, never set around feeling sorry for yourself that's fear that's a game that the Devil plays with your mind. James 4:7 Submit yourselves therefore to God. Resist the devil, and he will flee from you. Don't give him a room in your heart, don't let him rent a place in your house.

There is greatness on the inside of you stop sitting around waiting for someone to encourage you, greater is he that lives in you, than he that lives in the world.

The Bible tells us about a woman that had an issue of blood for twelve long years the bible didn't give her a name so you or I can put our name there. She had a problem while other women were having a good time enjoying life, she kept the faith, she presses her way she did not give up. She didn't let fear get her down, sometimes you have to press your way. Sometimes seem like you have to go through the storm of life for so long, problems in the home, problems on the job, problems after problems

This woman was weak, she didn't fear she kept the faith. Stir up your faith encourage yourself. No matter how limited our earthly possessions may be or how trying our circumstances, we never fear that God will desert or forsake us. Scripture declares that the heavenly Father cares for us. "The Lord is my helper, and I will not fear." Thou shalt fear the Lord thy God.

(Matthew 14:28-30) I want you to see this storm with your mind we have read about it, we have heard it preach many times. We have been through many storms, this morning the storm is raging; this is a severe storm. Trouble is all around them; it's dark it is hazy, it's about 3:00 a.m. in the morning. After feeding the multitudes, He had ordered His disciples to get into the boat and go ahead of Him to the other side while He sent the multitude away and to have a private prayer with God.

For hours these disciples are wrestling with this storm, the only authority that they have over this storm Is a voice of fear. The Devil smells fear when he can find a little doubt he will come in and work with your mind that old Devil will wear you out.

God has given us power love and a sound mind. The disciples were in the middle of a storm. The only thing they could think of if Jesus were here?

Watch Your Thoughts

Don't let no one pull you away from your dreams the dream God gives us has to go beyond wishful thinking. It has to become real on the inside of you. Anybody can talk about what they want to do or what they might do someday, you have got to pursue that dream. God had the bible put in print so that you and I could get an image of His promises, when we read it, we can visualize what He has said to us about our dreams. The more we hear the Word of God, the more the image of our dream is perfected within us. (Hebrews 11:9-10) By faith, Abraham sojourned in the land of promise as in a strange country dwelling in tabernacles with Isaac and Jacob the heirs with him of the same promise.

For he looked for a city which hath foundations whose builder and maker is God. He wants to be the Architect and the builder of your dreams. The reason why so many dreams fail is that you try to build them by yourself, you leave God outs of your plans.

No matter who you are or what your background is, God has a plan for your life. God is not just going around picking out a few people and dropping dreams in their hearts because He loves them more than He loves someone else. God wants to plant dreams in the hearts of every one of His children.

For a dream to drop into your heart, you've got to be in communion with God. You've got to have time and fellowship with Him. If you don't fellowship with Him, He will not fellowship with you.

It is easy to see other peoples blessings and ask "when is my dream coming true?". It is not wise to ask God for aid on your terms. It might not come to pass this week, or the next week, or even next year but keep the faith. No matter how long it takes.

Keep looking for it because you know that it is coming from God. Even when everything seems to go wrong, and our friends tell us it will never come to pass.

If you're not determined, fear will drag you down. When people tell you that you can't do it, stand on your faith. Abraham knew that God was the builder of dreams. We have to continually feed our spirit the Word of God to stay strong. We are never to give up, even if things look impossible. When you have a dream from God, you've got to be willing to keep it, you've got to be ready to press through fear.

Before the dream comes to pass, you may have to press through some obstacles. Some of those obstacles might have you crying at times, and some of those obstacles will have you on your knees calling on Jesus. We have got to stand through trials and tribulations. (1 Peter 1:7) That the testing of your faith, being much more precious than of gold that perisheth, though it is tried with fire, might be found unto praise and honor and glory at the appearing of Jesus Christ. [John 16:33) These things I have spoken unto you, that in me ye might have peace. In the world ye shall have tribulation: but be of good cheer; I have overcome the world.

When things seem wrong in your life: Paul said in(Philippians 3:13-14) Brethren, I count not myself to have apprehended: but this one thing I do, forgetting those things which are behind, and reaching forth unto those things which are before,(vs. 14) I press toward the mark for the prize of the high calling of God in Jesus Christ

Paul said I press on, his faith was his shield and his fuel for his journey. Sometimes you may get down, and feel a little depressed. Sometimes it appears that your blessing will never come. Remind yourself God blesses me every day. As he brought me victories in the past, he will empower me again. Get out of my way, fear. God has touched all our lives. If nothing more than healing a headache or putting food on your table.

When the devil says no, Remember he has no say in your faith or your reward. If God blesses you once He will bless you twice. He will bless you over and over if you keep the faith and don't' fear.

We need to watch our thoughts many times we are our worst enemy. That's the reason Paul told us in the Word that we are to be selective about our thoughts. (2 Cor. 10:5) Casting down imaginations and every high thing that exalteth itself against the knowledge of God and bringing into captivity every thought to the obedience of Christ.

Sometimes we claim things because we want them, but that is not what God wants us to have. When we don't get what we want, we lose our faith, we get upset. We start worrying, we doubt, and here comes fear. We begin to feel sorry for our self, the devil has you just where He wants you. You may be thinking I never had anything right happen in my life, You are still breathing. That is the first gift in a long line of rewards you must start to count. Without recognizing Gods influence in your life, your faith might not be able to carry you on.

The Bible says let everything that has breath praise the Lord. Think about all the things God has done for you. He has given you salvation. You may have needed healing, or you may have required a financial breakthrough, and He gave it to you. Focus on what God has already done, then things won't look so bad anymore.

(Habakkuk 2:3) For the vision is yet for an appointed time but at the end it shall speak and not lie, though it tarries wait for it because it will surely come, it will not linger

God's answer to him is the same answer He would give us. Be Patient I will work out my plans in my perfect timing. It isn't easy to be patient. God has a plan for you that will come to fruition. If you're going to hear the plan you've got to communicate with God, just listen. You've got to shut yourself away into a quiet place to pray, and when you pray, listen to Him. There will be doubters trying to discourage you from moving forward, there is nothing impossible when you put your trust in the living God. Don't allow the words of negative people to influence your faith. The devil may tell you that you can't do what God has told you to do. If God brings you to it, He will bring you through it.

You have the assurance from the word of God that his vision for you shall come to pass. Sometimes you have to wait and be patient, God will bless at the right place and the right time. When I fall, I'm so glad that I can ask Jesus to forgive me.

In spite of my shortcomings. Jesus still loves me. What is wrong with the world today? No LOVE! We have got to take up our cross and follow Jesus.

It's not easy at all, but, it was not easy for Jesus as he fell with the Cross on his back.

Jesus shows his love for us. Can't we show respect for one another? God wants us in everything. Give thanks for this is the will of God in Christ Jesus concern you (1 Thessalonians 5:17-18). It is seen strange that a man in prison would tell the church to rejoice. Paul's attitude teaches us a valuable lesson. Our inner attitude does not have to reflect on our outward circumstances. Paul was full of joy because he knew that no matter what happened to him, Jesus was with him.

It is so easy to get discouraged about unpleasant circumstances or to take unimportant events too seriously. Remember, during turmoil, God is still good. Watch your thoughts, instead of planning to get even with those people who mistreat you, do good to them. God is a father to us He forgives and forgets, and he wiped our record clean if we are following Him.

God is always thinking about us He cares about us, and we should put Him first in our lives. When insight is that when things don't fall perfectly into place, it doesn't mean that God is not working things out. It means his ways are not our ways some time we have to go through the darkness before God fix it. As we grow in our walk with the Lord, the water is often deeper.

He knows us intimately He knows every small problem you are worried about, and every single burden you have. When you approach Him for help He has all the time for you as if no one else exists, you have Him right by yourself. He is with us through every situation and in every trial, He is protecting us, loving us, guiding us. He orders our steps each and every day.

CHAPTER 5

Never Give Up

(**M**atthew 16:24-25) If any man will come after I let him deny himself and take up his cross and follow me. For whosoever will save his life shall lose it, and whosoever will lose his life for my sake shall find it.

God wants to be the architect and builder of our dreams. The reason why so many goals fail is that we take over and try to build them ourselves, we leave God out of our plans. We need to watch out thoughts many times we are our worth enemy. When Jesus used this picture of his followers taking up their crosses to follow him, the disciples know what he meant.

Crucifixion was a common Roman method of execution, and condemned criminals had to carry their crosses through the streets to the execution site. Following Jesus, therefore, meant a true commitment to the risk of death and no turning back. When we begin to live a life of faith and to follow our dreams, adversity is sure to arise because for the first time you're in danger to the adversary (Satan) because of your commitment to follow God.

When you make up your mind to follow Jesus, two will begin to happen immediately.

Your faith will grow, a major part of following Jesus is to stay in His Word, and listen to His voice; this will create a spirit of hope within, this will help you stand against the Devil.

The Devil comes to steal away all that you have received from God and His Word.

Your faith is a threat to the Devil he knows that if you are determined to walk in faith, then there is nothing he can do to stop you from receiving what God wants you to have. When trouble comes, it is often very tempting to drop your faith and pick up fear.

(1 John 5:4) Tells us for whatsoever is born of God overcometh the world, and this is the victory that overcometh the World, even our faith. Our faith is the victory that overcomes the world. That means that any attack by the Devil can be defeated when we walk in faith. There is simply nothing he can do to stop us. Sickness cannot stop us. The faith of God in us is greater than anything Satan can throw at us.

God can do far more in you and me than the Devil can do against us. God is greater than any challenge that comes your way. This is why we need to look to Him when things are too difficult for us to handle on our own. If you are in a situation where things seem totally impossible, then you are in good company. The apostle Paul also faced things that were beyond his ability, he was one of the greatest men of faith who ever lived. He said in (2 Corinthians Ch 1:9-10) But we had the sentence of death in ourselves, but we should not trust in ourselves, but in God which raiseth the dead. Who delivered us from so great a death and doth deliver in whom we believe that He will yet deliver us.

Why did Paul write this? He wanted us to understand the trouble he faced is that he knew that one in whom he trusted was greater than any pain. Paul was in a very critical situation, fear could have quickly taken over, but he kept the faith. He was involved in something that was beyond his own strength to overcome.

Have you ever found yourself in a situation where you know that you were not smart enough to figure out how to overcome it? The first thing we must learn to do when we feel as though things are more than we can bear, it time to stop trusting in our self, believe in God. A lot of people say that they are trusting God, you hear them saying I pray and I prayed I am going through, I am tired, I am so discouraged. Let me help somebody, Jesus tells us in (Matthew ch 10:38) to take up our cross and follow Him, means to be willing to identify with Him, being ready to face suffering publicly. When we're trusting God, there should be some excitement about the universe. We should be happy to tell people that you have decided to trust the provider and healer the shepherd and the deliverer. No one who truly trusts God ever loses.

That is why when we pray, pray in faith, we can go on and thank God for hearing your prayers. We don't want to pray in fear afraid God won't answer us we don't want that kind of relationship with God. A person who lives the life of faith lives an exciting experience. Who else do we know, who is as dependable, stable and unchanging as our God. Sometimes we fail to keep our promises to Him, He never fails us, we can always trust God. Paul said that he faced a situation in which he could not trust himself. When it comes to your dream your blessing, you have to get to the point where believing in yourself is not an option. Paul said that his trust was in God. He not only declared what God could do he also declared what God would do for him.

Paul said God will yet deliver us that's where we have to get in our faith God can, and God will bless you.

Paul said (2Corinthians 1:9) we felt like we'd been sent to death row that it was all over for us. As it turned out, it was the best thing that could have happened. When severe afflictions occur in our lives, we ought not to feel that God has forsaken us or has ceased to love us. We have to remind ourselves that these very things happened to God's faithful servants before us.

God allows trials so that He might come near to us. Let me help somebody, Paul went through so much, but he kept the faith. People will keep you from your dream. When God gives you a goal it is because He is calling you to do something for His glory throughout the scriptures, we know that we can do nothing without God working through us. Our strength and our possibilities are limited. There is nothing that cannot be accomplished when God is moving through a person who has faith in Him.

It does not matter how difficult things seem right now God can bring you through every situation. He will give you peace, joy, and happen. God is the God of all comfort; what does that mean? The picture we get of comfort is when we're feeling sorry for people who are experiencing trouble.

(2 Corinthians 1 3:4) Blessed be God, even the Father of our Lord Jesus Christ the Father of Mercies and the God of all comfort. God comforts us in all our tribulation that we may be able to comfort them, which are in any trouble. By the comfort wherewith, we are comforted of God. God wants you to draw near to those who are afflicted.

God comforts you in all your tribulations, He is willing to be our comforter in life no matter what you go through God will provide. He gives you the GRACE to help others in times of need. He comforts you so that you can bring that same comfort to others who may be facing tribulation.

If you are facing a situation that seems overwhelming, don't give up. Just like God has given you victory in the past, He will do it again. God will rescue you as many times as you need to be saved. God has an excellent track record, He has never failed. As long as we keep the FAITH and do not get fearful. This is why we have no need to worry.

When you face an impossible-looking situation that doesn't mean it's hopeless, that doesn't mean it's all over, and the Devil wins. It means that you are now in a position where you must trust God. Jesus tells us in (Matthew 6:34) Take, therefore, no thought for the morrow for the morrow shall take the view for the things of itself, sufficient unto the day is the evil thereof.

We focus on the things that we have not seen happen but ignore what God has already done. That is what the devil wants. He wants us to forget about the fact that we are still called and anointed to do what God wants us to do. He wants you and me to forget about all that God has already done in our lives.

Satan wants you to worry about all of the things that you have not seen happen yet. He wants you to ignore the fact that God is working behind the scene. God is doing things right now behind the view that you are not even aware of because He has promised that your due season is coming. While you're sitting there thinking that there is nothing else you can do God is working, and He will bless you because your due season is at hand,

The Devil wants you to worry about what might happen tomorrow. He does want you to live your life worrying day after day, week after week year after year. Just wondering whether or not God will do what He said He would do.

Paul said to rejoice in the Lord always, and again, I say enjoy. Rejoice in the Lord every day all day long even when you are facing trails, God wants you to shout and to praise Him. As long as JESUE is JESUS, and you have the words, you can speak it, then you can rejoice. It's not over until God says it's over. Enjoy every day that God wakes you up, He did not wake you up to worry and give the Devil your time. But to praise and glorify Him. It is time for you to stop walking around, looking discouraged and confused. It's time for you to make the devil discouraged and confused.

You are the one with the dreams and the vision, you are the one whom God has called. The only things the Devil can do is attempt to steal what God has given you, and he can't even do that if you don't let him. Quit focusing on what's not happening and start focusing on what is happening. We have to give our undivided attention to what God is doing right now.

Don't get worked up about what may or may not happen tomorrow. (Matthew ch 5) Jesus teaches His disciples a lesson on what to do when things get difficult.

1. Blessed are the poor in spirit for theirs is the kingdom of heaven.
2. Blessed are they that mourn for they shall be comforted.
3. Blessed are the meek for they shall inherit the earth.

When you are at the end of your rope, you are going to have to set aside your way of doing things and embrace God's way of doing things. When we lay aside our own feelings, our own way of responding to trouble. God will take over from there. When a problem comes, we always get fearful, keep the FAITH.

The same faith that Paul had to use is the same Faith that is on the inside of you and I. The same God, David depended on lives inside of you and I. The solution is not worrying we often run everywhere looking for the answer. The solution is to spend some time with Jesus what Jesus was saying if you want real rest then get always with me. And watch how I work. I won't let you down. If you are at the end of your rope, then it's time for you to get away with Jesus. Spend more time with Him when you spend time with Jesus. Don't talk about your problems He knows your issues let Him speak to you what we do is exposed to God, so we don't have to go to Him crying and worrying. He already knows what we're going through. He already knows the pressure you're under, you are not going to surprise Him with anything. There's no reason to sit there crying and in fear about problems. Jesus knows all of your aching and pains.

Just go before God and say to him I've come to get away with you. I want to spend some time with you. I want to get closer to you I want to get to know you better, Jesus just you and me when you pray set there for a little while, medicate then open your bible and read when you open it, you will open it to what God is telling you.

God called Abraham a father before he actually became a father. God was calling things that were not as though they were. The promise (or Covenant) God gave Abraham, said that Abraham would be the father of many nations. The entire world would be blessed through him. The promise was fulfilled in Jesus Christ, you see Jesus was from Abraham's line, and the whole world was blessed through him. Abraham never fears he never doubted that God would fulfill his promise. He walks by faith.

Don't get Abraham wrong, his life was not perfect, His life was marked by mistakes by, sin and failures. But he also had wisdom and goodness he trusted God. His faith was strengthened by the obstacles he faced. Abraham looked to God he obeyed God and just waited for God to fulfill His WORD.

So just tell the Devil taking his hands off you Jesus said that I am his if Jesus says it's mind if He says I can have it then it's mind. The only person who can stop your dream from happening is you. How? By getting weary and giving up.

CHAPTER 6

When I Fall, I Shall Arise

(M)icah 7:7-8) Therefore I will look unto the Lord I will wait for the God of my salvation my God will hear me.

Rejoice not against me O mine enemy when I fall I shall arise when I sit in darkness the Lord shall be a light unto me. In step 1, No one is without mistake we've all stumbled, we've all fallen at some time or another. In fact, we will probably make a few more mistakes along the way. Always remember it's not failure to fall, it's only failure to stay down. When you fall, the Devil expects you to quit. He wants you to say where is God. When God calls you to do something you better do it.

Notice how positive Micah was when he faced trials. He did not allow His difficulty to keep him down. He was not one to fall down and to stay down. He let the enemy know that even if things seemed to be dark and difficult, He would trust in God and allow Him to be a light unto Him. It's Amazing Christians look everywhere but to the Lord for their answers. There are so many people he ignores the very one they need, Jesus is our answer.

Micah said I will look unto the Lord, That's the smartest thing that you can do when nothing seems to be working. Keep your eyes on Jesus. He knows what to do, and He will reveal it to you. God wants us to look to Him, He wants us to stop trying to find answers for ourselves and be prepared to receive as we look to Him. Be patient, his answer will come.

Micah proclaimed that he would look to the Lord and wait on the God of his salvation. There are times when things happen instantly in my personal walk of faith most of the time that has not been the case. I've had some miracles that have arrived almost as quickly as I could speak the prayer out of my mouth. I've seen miracles at the very moment I prayed for people. The majority of the time I've had to wait on the Lord. We live between Amen, and there it is. The moment we pray, we believe we receive.

Then we start our walk of faith to reach there it is often the period between Amen, and there it is. This long and we have no other choice but to wait until we see the manifestation. I made a decision a long time ago that I will not give up, no matter how long it takes. You might be wondering how long do I have to wait until my dream becomes a reality, that answer to that is simple. You wait until it happens, no matter how long it seems to take. What is important is that you make the decision to stay in faith.

Notice Micah did not say I'll try. He said I will if you're going to keep the faith then it has to be on the act of your will it's not something you try it is something you deliberately will do. If you tell yourself that you will try to live by faith, what the Devil hears is that you're not committed yet. What the Devil here coming out of your mouth is I'm not sure that this will work, Micah didn't say I'll try to wait on the God of my salvation. He said I will wait; we must have patience when we pray.

Will, your spiritual ears are attentive to His voice when He speaks, what if He tells you to continue to stand on His Word will you be obedient? Will you wait for your dream no matter how long it takes. Don't let the Devil steal your vision, your future is not in the Devil's hands. It is in the hands of the God of your Salvation. Some people think there dream will come the right time they except Jesus Christ God paid dearly with the life of his son He paid the highest price he could pay.

Jesus paid the price, so when we fall He loves us so much we can ask forgiveness, he accepted our punishment He paid the price for our sins. He paid the price so we can love one another just like he love us.

Check Your Oil
The Bridegroom Is Coming

Jesus gave the following parables to clarify further what it means to be ready for his return and how to live until he comes. In this parable of the bridesmaids, we are taught that every person is responsible for His or her own spiritual condition. I'm lead by the Word of God to believe it will happen just like it did during the time of Noah's, people did not believe. They went on doing whatever they wanted to do the day Noah entered the Art they still did not believe.

On the wedding day, the bridegroom went to the bride's house for the ceremony. Then the bride and the groom along with a grand parade returned to the groom's house where a feast took place. The virgins were waiting for them, and they hoped to take part in the wedding banquet, but when the groom didn't come at the expected time, five of them were out the oil. These five foolish virgins were good, but they didn't know Jesus Christ as Lord and Savior. The Bible said they were on there a way to the wedding they did not think about what time it was. The foolish virgins didn't stop to check their oil. The five virgins had oil in their lamps, A child of God keep oil they are ready to do the will of God.

While the bridegroom tarried they all slumbered and slept, the Bible tells us around midnight someone cried out Behold the Bridegroom is coming. They all got up the five wise had checked their oil, they had enough oil to meet Jesus. The five foolish did not have enough oil to meet Jesus, their light was gone out. Ever now and then you need to check your oil make sure everything is fine with you and God. The foolish wanted some of the wise oil.

The wises told them we just have enough for ourselves go to the store and buy for yourself. Why the foolish was going to buy oil, Jesus came the wise was ready they went into heaven with Jesus. When Jesus returns to take his people to heaven, we must be prepared. Spiritual preparation cannot be bought or borrowed at the minute. Our relationship with God must be our own every day of my life. I am packing up getting ready to meet Jesus. It will be a sad, sad day to get to heaven doors and can't go in. To look at Jesus in the face and can't go back with him. When the foolish virgins got back, the door has been closed. And no one could get in. The foolish give us some of your oil, too late, Let us in too late the wedding is over. It will be a sad day when Jesus say depart from me, I don't know you we got to leave this word this is not our home.

When you feel down, you may find difficult to give thanks take heart –God works all things out for good if we love him and are fitting into his plans thank God, not for your problems but for the strength he is building in you through the painful experiences of your life. You can be sure that God's perfect love will see you through. This doesn't mean that God will take away all our troubles. The real test is our faith, see if we can stand up for Christ in spite of our problems.

Forget those things which are behind you, our goal is to know Jesus Christ. To be like him and to be all he had in mind for us. This is an excellent example for every Christian stop Pulling the same old jump from day to day, let go and let God. Run the race with the patient. (Ephesians 5:6) Let no man deceive you with vain words. All of us know the pains of betrayal in best friends, a wife or a husband, or a child is just a family member.

What does it take to be able to say Lord let your will be done, it seeks to trust in God's plans, prayer, and obedience each step of the way, and it takes patience? If our FAITH is reliable, we don't need to be afraid of what lies ahead. The Devil is defeated by God no matter how powerful he becomes or how terrible our situation seems, God is in control, and He will be victorious. Our task is to be prepared for Christ and to spread the good News, help others that don't know Him. When God forgives our sins, our record is wiped clean, (Psalm 103:12) When we ask forgiving God will put out sins away from us as far as the East is from the West. When we accept Jesus Christ as our Savior, an exchange takes place. We give Christ Jesus our sins, and he forgives us and makes us right with God.

You might know somebody that wants to come to Jesus, but his or her sins they think are too many. Tell that person that while Jesus died on the cross so we can have the right to the tree of life. You remember the hymn Amazing Grace How sweet the sound that saved a wretch like me. I once was lost, but now I'm found I was blind, but now I see. At some time in all our lives, we were blind but thank GOD now I see.

Someone might be thinking I have so many problems in my life, I feel like I'm so broken. If it not one thing it is another can I tell you that I been there, I just held on to His hand? When I held on to his hand, He held on to me, that is a great feeling to hold on to JESUS hand your miracles are coming out of holding on.

Sometimes we have to mix faith and patience together and wait some time it takes the patient a while to get there don't give up keep the faith, He will come on his timing. Please be patient, we are running some time we fall, but we get up, brush yourself off, ask God to forgive us. Sometime with tears in our eyes, we wipe them away and keep on running. We can enter directly into God's presence through prayer. I was welcome, with open arms because we are his children someone is thinking I been praying for a long time and He has not answered me, where is your faith? God did not say he would come at every call, be patient keep the faith He is worth waiting on. So many times, while waiting for that old Devil tries to change your mind, telling you that God does not love you, He is not going to answer your prayer. Tell that old Devil I am patiently waiting on God. I prayed last week God wants to answer me while you are waiting on God keep the faith be patient while you are waiting trust him and wait on him. God will never let you down, He might not answer your prayers the way you want him to, but he knows what best for you.

Come boldly to the throne of grace that we may obtain mercy and find grace to help in time of need. If you are going to doubt don't pray, come boldly, unto the throne of grace that you may obtain mercy and find grace to help in the of need. Don't be afraid to ask him to meet your demand; he is the best friend you will ever have.

Our clean consciences allow us to enter God's presence with boldness we have asked God to forgive us, faith said he did if it come from the heart. We are like an athlete we have got to train hard and run well, we have to remember the reward is at the end. Two words describe our faith, confidence, and certainty. The beginning point of faith is believing in God's character. He is who he says he is, hold on to your belief we all have been through some kind of storm. Storm makes us stronger, makes us pray and make us humble.

If you have not had a storm in your life, can I tell you just to wait awhile? We all are going to have storms in our lives; I don't care how rich you are or how poor you are storms are coming. One good thing about it, we cannot pay our way to heaven. Jesus is always with us, but he might not stop your storm today is next week.

The Word of God he rebuked the wind and the raging water they ceased, and everything was calm. Jesus said to them, where is your Faith. Who wouldn't serve a God like this, the wind and the water obey him, with little warning storms can come in our life they can go so quit without warning, we can go to bed at night sleep great, get up the next morning happy feeling good, but the next night we can be so sad because a storm wind blew in our house. You didn't see no lighting, you did here no thunder all you got was the rain the tears that fall from your eyes.

Don't be like the disciples they didn't know Jesus could control the storms, Jesus controls storms of nature, and he controls our troubled hearts, we can make sure our faith stays strong by getting back to the principles of the love of God. We can develop the kind of faith by turning our passion and confidence outward to help and benefit others. To do that we'll have to forget about ourselves. The highest goal you could ever have in this life is to help others.

Faith brings hope into reality and gives substance to it. (Hebrews 11:1) says, "Now faith is the substance of things hoped for, the evidence of things not seen." The object of hope becomes a reality through faith. Hope is always in the future, trust is still now. The Scripture is the basis of your prayers. The Word of Jesus Christ tells us: If we confess with our mouth Jesus Christ as Lord and you believe in your heart that God has raised Him from the dead; God's Word says ask him to forgive you for your sins you are saved.

Prayer for healing is the same faith principles search God's Word for your answer. (Isaiah 53:5) says, 'But he was wounded for our transgressions, He was bruised for our iniquities; the chastisement of our peace was upon him, and by His stripes, we are healed." (Matthew 8:17 says, "Himself took our infirmities and bared our sicknesses.

Once you have prayed hold fast to your confession, refuse to speak contrary to the Word of God. Do not allow circumstances to sway you, act as though it were already done. When you apply your faith accurately according to God's Word, you will get results. You will experience (Hebrews 4:16) for yourself. "Let us, therefore, come boldly unto the throne of grace, which we may obtain mercy, and find grace to help in time of need." If you believe that GO on and say AMEN.

If God answers the prayer of a sinner to be saved, He will

certainly answer the prayer of born-again believers who come to Him in faith concerning their lives. Faith and Fear, you cannot function in both at the same time. In praying effectively, a vital part of your success is knowing how to refuse doubt, fear, and unbelief.

Doubt operates in the mental realm, God's Word operates in the spiritual realm. Our responsibility is to use the spiritual weapons at our disposal. For though we walk in the flesh we do not war after the flesh: (For the weapons of our warfare are not carnal, but mighty through God to the pulling down of strongholds). Casting down imaginations, and every high thing that exalteth itself against the knowledge of God, and bringing into captivity every thought to the obedience of Christ.

Satan uses doubt and fear to bluff you into accepting defeat, you can overcome him by the power of God and faith in His word. You can avoid failure by preparing to succeed once you have prayed in faith; you must stand your ground until the manifestation comes. Fight the good fight of faith, stand firm on the Word, and believe God results, allow Him to do something with your circumstances. God is on your side! Prepare to succeed not to fail, when you pray in Jesus' Name, according to the Word in Faith, God will quickly respond to you (John 16:23).

We pray for healing then think, what will I do if God does not heal me? Maybe I had better get an appointment with the doctor. He is very busy this time of the year, I might not be able to see him. Then if God does not heal me, I will be in a mess. With that attitude, believing God will be a waste of time. The person who thinks that way will be unable to receive from God. That is FEAR before he prays he is already preparing to fail, he does not have any faith he is double minded and, according to (James 1:8) unstable in all his ways. The man who wavers in his mind will never receive from God, he is like a wave of the sea driven with the wind and tossed about in every direction. He has a backup plan, "just in case." The moment he feels the least bit sick, he will operate in Fear and unbelief

He is thinking, what am I going to do if I fail? If you have a setback, just get back in the Word of God. The power of God is the same, whether you feel like it or not. Receive the Word into your heat.

Renew your mental attitude to the Word Prepare to succeed, and you will receive the manifestation in the physical realm.

CHAPTER 7

Check Your Armor

Our responsibility is to stand ground as a soldier in Christ, wearing our spiritual armor. Put on the hold armor of God (Ephesians 6:13-17). Paul was talking about spiritual wickedness. He is coming to the end of the epistle, in his conclusion, he said to be strengthened in the Lord and in the power of his might.

Satan has a well-organized group, the heartbreak, the heartache, he is the cause of the significant problems that are in the world today. Many churches have lost sight of the spiritual battle. We feel that if we have a lovely church building, and attracting big crowds and if the finances are coming in, everything is going right. The battle is the Word of God Being taught. In the Christian life, we battle every day against Principalities and powers. The powerful evil forces of fallen angels headed by Satan. And to withstand their attacks, we must depend on God's strength and use every piece of his armor.

Paul is giving this to all individuals within the church. The holding body needs to be armored me help somebody, lions attack sick, young or straggling animals they choose victims who are alone or not alert. If you are feeling alone weak helpless and cut off from other believers. Or if you are so focused on your troubled that you forget to watch for the danger, these are the times when you are especially vulnerable to Satan's attacks.

During times of suffering seek other Christians for support don't get fearful keep your eyes on Jesus. And resist the devil. The Devil wants us to think that our dream will never come to pass, and become discouraged the only was a child of God would have the right to be discouraged if Jesus was no longer Lord and the word was no longer valid. Jesus is Lord for all of eternity, and the word of God shall forever be true.

You may be facing the worst crisis that you've ever experienced, but it's not over yet. We got to learn how to look at things the way God sees them. The way God sees them may be much different from the way that we see them. It may seem as if you have lost everything, it may look as if you will never get over all the attacks that have been launched against you. You may have been through the storm I want you to notice one thing, you are still standing, and for this reason, it is time to rejoice.

The Devil may have hit you with his best shot. You are still standing you must not give up. Keeping trusting in God keep declaring the word of God over your situation. It time to rejoice you have the Devil right where you want him, so straighten up your armor and tell that Devil you will not quit.

Keep standing the victory is yours. Paul said I was able to stand against the wiles of the Devil. In the Christian life, we battle against principalities and power. To withstand their attacks, we must depend on God strength and use every piece of his armor. Paul is giving this counsel to every individual within the church. The whole body needs to be armed.

Sometimes you may feel as though your armor is falling off, maybe you don't even know where your helmet is. This is not the time to start stripping off your armor keep it on tighten it up and stand. We have got to base our faith on what God said He says that all things are possible to them who believe.

(Matthew 14:25-27), Said in the fourth watch of the night

Jesus went unto them walking on water. When the disciples saw him walking on water, they were troubled, saying it is a spirit they cried out for fear.

But straightway Jesus spake unto them saying be of good cheer it is I be not afraid the disciples had been told to go to the other side a great storm had arisen, and the board was filling with water. The disciples believed they were all about to drown; they all were fearful where were there faith?

The Bible says that in the fourth watch of the night, Jesus came, saying it is I be not afraid. The fourth watch of the night is the darkest part of twenty hours. Most people think it's midnight but it's not, it's always the darkest just before the dawn.

You may be in the fourth watch of the night your boat may be filled with water and waves may be beating against your ship. It may look to you as if there is no way to go but down. When your storm of life gets terrible to keep the faith, Jesus will always come in your darkest hour.

When you are in your darkest hour seem like things will never be right anymore, you think about giving up. That's when you can start looking for the Lord, He will be there with you no matter how dark things seem. The disciples did not recognize Jesus when he started toward them. They were afraid, They even cried out saying, "it is a spirit." Finally, Jesus said, "be of good cheer it is I." Most people don't recognize Jesus in their darkest hour because they are not looking for Him. Jesus is walking toward you today. He has your miracle in his hands.

In our Christian life, we battle against "principalities and power" (Ephesians 6:10-12). Paul tells you to be strong in the LORD, in the power of his might. Put on the whole armor of God, that ye may be able to stand against the wiles of the devil. For we wrestle not against flesh and blood, but against principalities, against power, against the rulers of the darkness of this world, against spiritual wickedness in high places.

In the Christian life, we battle against "principalities and power" (the mighty evil forces of fallen angels headed by Satan, who is a vicious fighter. To withstand their attacks, we must depend on God's strength and use every piece of his or her armor. Paul is not only giving this counsel to the church, the body of Christ, but to all individuals within the church.

The whole body needs to be armed. As you do battle against "the rulers of the darkness of this world." Fight in the strength of the church, whose power comes from the Holy Spirit, those who are not "flesh and blood" are demons over whom Satan has control. They are not mere fantasies—they are very real. We are facing a powerful army whose goal is to defeat Christ's church.

When we believe in Christ and join his church, these beings become our enamine, and they try every device to turn us away from Christ and back to sin. Although we are assured of victory, we must engage in the struggle until Christ comes, because Satan is constantly battling against all who are on the Lord side. We need supernatural power to defeat Satan, and God has provided that in his Holy Spirit within us and his armor surrounding us. If you feel discouraged to remember Jesus' words to Peter: ' Upon this rock, I will build my church, and the gates of hell shall not prevail it,

Our responsibility is to stand out as a soldier in Christ, wearing our Spiritual Armor. Put on the hold armor of God. Paul was coming to an end, in his conclusion, he tells us to be strengthened in the Lord, and in the power of his might. Many people have lost sight of the spiritual battle, we feel that if we have a lovely home, beautiful car, and a big bank account, everything is going right. The struggle is, the Word of God being taught are we living God Word. Are do we just go to church on Sunday or whatever day and doing the week we live like we want to live. We must realize that there is spiritual warfare being carried on today. We are living in a time now we need the LORD. We need to be grounded in the Word of God, not only rooted in his Word, but also living his Word. We must depend on God's strength and use every piece of his armor.

(1 Peter 5:8) Be sober, because of your adversary the Devil, as a roaring lion, walketh about seeking whom he may devour. The lions attack sick young or straggling animals. They choose victims who are alone or not alert. Peter warns us to watch out for Satan when we are suffering or persecuted. These are the times when you are especially vulnerable to Satan's Attacks. He knows that his time is limited. I've learned that when the greatest pressure comes on me to quit. That's a good indication that Satan just fired his best shot and if that one doesn't get you, then he's finished. There have been times in my life where it seemed the more I prayed, the worse things got, Jesus was carrying me. I find myself asking Jesus, what do you want me to do? He said to stand on my Word.

Take unto you the whole armor of God, that ye may be able to withstand in the evil days and having done all to stand. After doing everything that we know to do, we must continue to stand no matter how difficult thing appears. God will not let us lose this battle, our responsibility as believers are to stand our ground as a soldier in Christ wearing all your spiritual armor. Not only are we to be in a standing position, but we are also to have on a specific helmet to protect ourselves. Now we are told to be girded with truth in the face of the enemy.

Truth is that which holds everything together; it is the word of God. Paul has already told us to put on Christ he is the one who is the truth, and we should put him on in our lives. Put on the whole armor of God that ye may be able to stand against the wiles of the Devil. Put on the breastplate of righteousness, Jesus Christ is the righteousness one. Your feet shod with the preparation of the gospel of peace. Shoes are necessary for standing.

In hand to hand combat, they were taught to make sure their feet were anchored. Above all, taking the shield of faith. The protection covered all of the armor, faith enables us to enter the door. I am the door, if any man comes in, he shall be saved. My sheep hear my voice, and I know them, and they follow me, and I give unto them eternal life. And they shall never perish neither shall any man pluck them out of my hand.

Take the helmet of salvation, the helmet protects the head, God appeals to the mind of man The word of God called the sword of the spirit the word of God is quick it's powerful and sharper than any two-edged sword. There was a time in my life I felt that I just could not stand any longer. I felt as if I had held for so long that my armor was falling off.

When the attacks first started, my sword was sharp, my shield was strong all the rest of my armor was intact. I felt as if my breastplate was falling off, my shield of faith was so heavy that I could not hold it up any longer. I could not even see the enemy because my helmet had slipped down over my eyes. I asked God, what do I do now? He said to stand on God Word.

You May have been through the storm, and you think God does not hear your prays, Jesus will step on board and ride the storm out with us. But you are still standing you have a reason to rejoice. Thank God I was able to stand against the wiles of the Devil.

In this Christian life, we battle against principalities and power, to withstand their attacks, we must depend on God's strength and use every piece of his armor. Sometime you may feel as though your armor is falling off. Maybe you don't even know where your helmet is. This is not the time to start stripping off your armor, keep it on and tighten it up and stand. If you have to stand by your self stand on God Word.

Stand firm don't let nobody turn you around, stand on God Word be ready when Christ returns Stand firm because we know Christ is coming live each day to please God don't worry about pleasing man. Please, God, not man, man don't have nowhere to put you. If anybody asks you why are you holding on tell them when we stand firm on God word, it builds up our faith.

Through your troubles stand, pain and sorrow, stand firm, David said I will bless the Lord at all times. Stand firm Jesus stood firm for you and I. When you are going through trials sometimes it not for you, it's for someone else to get there soul right with Jesus. Sometimes God uses people to help us grew you do not put in the towel and say I quit.

You must realize that there is spiritual warfare being carried on today. When you are on the battlefield, waiting for God to help us is not easy. But it is worth waiting for. The prize of the high calling of God in Christ Jesus, the prize is not some earthly reward but is to catch up and be in the presence of Christ Jesus.

(Ephesians 6:10-17) Paul talks about being a soldier for the Lord, he tells us that we cannot overcome the Devil ourselves, you and I are no match for the Devil we are not even told to fight the Devil, we are told that God will fight for us.

Paul said to be strong in the Lord and in the power of his might, put on the hold armor of God so that ye may be able to stand. Satan has a well-organized group, a well-organized family, and a well-organized friend and a well-organized church. The heartbreak, the heartaches, the suffering the tragedies of life are the work of Satan in the background. He is the cause of the great problems that are in the world today. We are to stand, not only are we to stand, but we are also to have our armor to protect ourselves.

We are told to be girded with truth in the face of the enemy that truth is the Word of God. If you don't have on the armor of God, then you are spiritually weak. The breastplate protects the organs in the chest area from the enemy. Without the breastplate, we will be defeated. The feet shoes are necessary for standing, we need a good solid foundation your feed needs to be anchored on the rock.

Above all, taking the shield of faith, faith is dependence on God His presence on His power. Faith puts God between you and the enemy. Take the helmet of salvation. The helmet protects the head, God does appeal in the minds of men. Be a good soldier for Christ Jesus, there is a time to fight, and there time to stand still. We are a soldier on the battlefield, on every battlefield you have some enemies.

CHAPTER 8

I'M Never along

J esus says we can ask for anything, but we must remember that our asking must be in his name. We cannot use his name as a magic formal to fulfill our selfish desires. If we are sincerely following God. And seeking to do his will, then our request will be in line with what he wants, and he will grant it to you.

We see here that Jesus was soon going to leave the disciples, but he would remain with them, how could this be? I AM WITH YOU. This promise is Christ's assurance to those involved in winning the lost and teaching them to observe His righteous standards. Jesus arose, is now alive, and is now live, and is personally interested in each one of His children. He is with us in the person of the Holy Spirit.

(John 14:15-16)' If ye love me, keep my commandments. And I will pray for the Father, and he shall give another Comforter, that he may abide with you forever; Jesus called the Holy Spirit another Comforter." "Comforter" translates the Greek meaning literally "one called alongside to help. This is a precious word, meaning Comforter, Strengthener, Counselor, Helper, Adviser, Advocate, Ally, and Friend. In other words, the Holy Spirit continues what Christ Himself did while on earth.

Jesus promises to send another Comforter. The Holy Spirit will do for the disciples what Christ did for them while He was with them. The Spirit will be by their side to help and strengthen them to teach the true course for their lives, to comfort in a difficult situation, to intercede in prayer for them to be a friend to further their best interest, and to remain with them forever. Therefore Jesus is our helper and intercessor in heaven while the Holy Spirit is our indwelling helper and intercessor on earth.

The Holy Spirit was sent so that God would be with and wit in all believes that follows after Jesus returned to heaven. His spirit would comfort us Guide us to know his truth

Jesus called the Holy Spirit another comforter, the one that alongside to help. We can call it the strengthener, The counselor, The Helper. The Teacher, The Adviser, The Advocate, and a Friend. After 40 days with the disciples, Jesus ascended into heaven. It was important for the disciple to see Jesus taken up into heaven so they would know without a doubt that he was God and his home was in heaven. Two angels told the disciples that one day, Jesus would return in the same way he had gone bodily and visibly.

The church must be ready for his sudden return. (John 14:17), even the spirit of truth whom the world cannot receive because it seeth him neither knows him, but ye know him for he dwelleth with you and shall be in you. To Abide in Christ mean believing he is God's Son receiving him as savior and lord by doing what God says, continuing in faith and loving one another.

Jesus says the only way to live a perfect life is to stay close to him. He wants His people to be Holy just as he is Holy. Set apart, different, unique, Christians are called to be Holy. Prayer is our approach to God, and we are to come boldly unto the throne of grace comes reverence, for he is our King, our Father, come with bold assurance He is our friend and counselor.

Do you ever feel like you don't know how to pray? We have the wonderful promise that we pray. The Holy Spirit intercedes for us according to the will of God. The time is near all signs point to the soon return of the Lord.

The time is running out, and destruction will soon be upon here, Time is running out. We don't know when our lives will end, don't let anything or anybody hold you back from God. One of my friends told me that she was on the battlefield for the Lord. But she did not have all her gifts to fulfill her mission. The Holy Spirit will not be the comforter of those who are indifferent to the faith.

The Holy Spirit will not help or live in half-hearted Christians. In their commitment to the truth, you have got to be real. He comes only to those who worship the Lord in spirit and in truth.

(1 John 4:18) There is no fear in love; but perfect love casteth out fear: because of fear hath torment. He that feareth is not made perfect I love.

If we are ever afraid of the future, the eternity of God's judgment., we can remind ourselves of God's love. We know he loves us perfectly. We can resolve our fears first by focusing on his immeasurable love for us, and then by allowing focusing on his endless love for us, and then by allowing him to love others through us. His love quiets your fears and gives you confidence. The power of the Holy Spirit can help us overcome our fear of what some might say or do to us we can continue to do God's work

(Hebrews 11:31) It is a Fearful thing to fall into the hands of the living God.

God's power is incredible, and his punishment terrible. These words give us a glimpse into the holiness of God. He is sovereign; his power is unlimited; he will do as he promises. This judgment is for those who have rejected God's mercy. For them. Falling into God's hands will be a terrible experience. They will have no more excuses. They will discover that they were wrong, but it will be too late. For those who accept Christ's love and accept his salvation. The coming judgment is no cause to worry. Being saved through his grace, they have nothing to fear.

(Revelation 3:16) So then because thou art lukewarm and

neither cold, and neither cold nor hot I will spew thee out of my mouth. Lukewarm means you still have the world on your mind that a person is wretched and miserable. Jesus warns such a person that he will reject them. (James 3:12) Can the fig tree bear Oliver or a grape bear figs? So can no fountain both yield salt water and fresh. What James is saying, a man can be a two-faced-double-minded man can mean both good and bad.

No fountain down here on this earth is going to give forth both sweet and bitter water, nor will a tree bear both figs and Olivers. What is dead faith? First, everyone has the hope of some kind. There are hundreds of religions in this world, and they all require faith, but they do not all require the faith that justifies. How can I know that my faith is the faith that justifies sinners? There is only one FAITH that saves, that is, faith in the saving life and work of Christ, the God-Man. All other hope is empty and dead

Paul taught "that a man is justified by FAITH with Christ ... {therefore} the life which I now live in the flesh I live by faith in the Son of God, who loved me and gave Himself for me. I was not set aside the grace of God {by adding the works of the law to God's grace}: for if righteousness comes through the law, then Christ died in vain."

A living faith, given by God. We do not live by faith that we generate, that is always dead, empty faith. The faith justifies id the gift of God. "For by grace, you have been saved through faith, and that not of yourselves; it (faith) is the gift of God, not of works, lest anyone should boast." This faith, God's gift. Can only be found through the infallible Word of God.

Jesus tells us in His Word that He will never leave us we want never be along. Through your Trial and tribulations, Jesus said I will be there. I will be your comforter, I will be your strengthener, I will be your best friend. God is concerned about every human being He creates, He's not willing that any should perish.

When we trust God, we walk with Him, we grow in grace, He carries our Burdens, He carries our sins, our shame {Matthew 18:

8). Wherefore if thy hand or thy foot offend thee, cut them off and cast them from thee, it is better for thee to enter into life halt or maimed rather then having two hands or two feet to be thrown into everlasting fire.

The Holy Spirit will do for you. Just like it did for the disciples, The spirit will be by your side and to comfort you. It intercedes in prayer for us. He will be with you forever, you are never along Jesus is our helper, our intercessor. Jesus lives in heaven, and He is interceding for you every day.

What is dead faith? Firth, everyone has the hope of some kind. There are hundreds of religions in this world, and they all require faith, but they do not all require the faith that justifies How can I know that my faith is the faith that justifies the sinner? There is the only faith that saves, that is, faith in the saving life and work of Christ, the God-Man (Gal. 2:20). All other faith is empty and dead. (Gal. 2:20) "I have been crucified with Christ it is no longer I who live, but Christ lives in me and the life which I now live in the flesh I live by the faith of the Son of God, who loved me and gave Himself for me. Pray by faith, when you ask anything from God in prayer, it must be by faith, there can be no doubting, for if you waver, you will not receive anything from the Lord. Always pray, keep the faith, believe, and trust Him, How can anyone pray all the time? One way to pray continually is to make quick, brief prayers your habitual response to every situation you meet with throughout the day.

Another way is to order your life around God's desires and teachings so that your very life becomes a prayer. You don't have to isolate yourself from other people and from daily work to pray continually. You can make prayer your life and your life a prayer living in a world that needs God's powerful influence.

You are never alone, God is always by your side if we let Him He will lead us all the way from earth to heaven. Some of the roads get bad, storms in our life but walk on. Every storm makes us stronger in the Lord.

God wants us to total surround to Him give him our all, sometimes the burden is so heavy, and you can't say a word all you can do is wave your hands. Praise is not to be held on the inside, let it go give God your praise, give him the glory. Stop holding on to those heavy burdens you carrying around, let go and let God.

The Lord is on your side, when you went through your storm, God never left you, he brought you through. The Lord is your strength, he is your refuge in troubled times, he is your shield in the time of a storm. God loves us He sent Jesus his only son to die for us. We can have eternal life through faith in him because he broke the power of death with his resurrection.

CHAPTER 9

STILL Away Just You Jesus

Get away with Jesus go in your secret closet and talk with Jesus, tell Him all about your problems not that He doesn't know about them because He does (Isaiah 43:26), God said put me remembrance: let us plead together: declare thou, that thou mayest be justified.

What are you saying God? Remind me of my promise to thee. (Psalm 51:3)" For I acknowledge my transgressions, and my sin is ever before me. No sin is too great to be forgiven! Do you feel that you could never come close to God because you have done something terrible? God can and will forgive you of any sin. While God forgives us, however, he does not always erase the natural consequences of our sin.

God has a way out of every situation that Satan has created to destroy us. Paul gave strong encouragement to the Corinthians about resisting temptation. Paul said temptation happen to everyone, so don't feel you've been singled out. He said others have resisted temptation and so can you. Paul said any temptation can be resisted because God will help you resist it.

You have got to recognize those people and situations that give you trouble

Run from anything you know is wrong.

Choose to do only what is right.

Pray for God's help.

See friends who love God and can offer help when you are tempted.

Paul said running from a tempting situation is your first step on the way to victory. The same people that try to pull you into temptation will mass your dream up. They are not going anywhere and if you stay around them. Running away is sometimes considered, cowardly, fear-wise people realize that removing themselves physically from temptation is often the most courageous action to take.

Paul warned the people to run from anything that produced evil thoughts. You've got to be sensitive to the Spirit of God for you to hear the instructions regarding the way of escape. We cannot keep company with a lot of carnal-minded people all the time. It's not good to sit around and worry about tomorrow, where is your faith.

(Matthew 17: 20). So Jesus said to them, "because of your unbelief; for assuredly, I say to you, if you have faith as a mustard seed, you will say to this mountain, 'Move from here to there, and it will move, and nothing will be impossible for you.

You have to create an atmosphere that will build your faith, not tear it down. Don't let fear get you down worrying about tomorrow. You have got to place yourself in a position where we can hear the instructions of God so He can show you the way out. Come unto me all ye that labor and are heavy laden, and I will give you rest. Take my yoke upon you and learn of me; for I am meek and lowly in heart, and ye shall find rest unto your soul. For my yoke is easy, and my burden is light. (Matthew 11:28-30).

Jesus frees people from all these burdens. The rest that Jesus promises is love, healing, and peace with God, not the end or all labor. A relationship with God changes meaningless toil into spiritual productivity and purpose. Responsibilities weigh us down, even the effort of staying faithful to God. But Jesus' yoke remains easy compared to the crushing alternative. I will allow no trouble, crisis, or suffering to shake my confidence in God. Not only from God come to our deliverance, but he is our salvation and our strength I had to learn to pray and tell him all that was in my heart, I thought that he would come on my time, but I learned that I had to wait on his timing. We have got to wait upon the Lord to act on our behalf. Trust in him at all times, pour out your heart before him, God is your refuge.

The wait is a word we hate to hear there are times God wants you to wait on Him for the right timing, we do not know what is best for us. We think we no! But we do not. Real relief does not come when the problem is solved, because more problems are always on the way. Real help comes from God alone when a situation seems out of control; we can trust God to do mighty things. Ask him to create in you a clean heart, God renews a right spirit within me.

Whither shall I go from thy Spirit or whither shall I flee from thy presence. If I ascend up into heaven, you are there, if I make my bed in Hell, you are there. If I take the wings of the morning and dwell in the uttermost parts of the sea, you are right there. When depressed by problems and struggling. We can not get away from God, Be encouraged that God keeps you in His thoughts. He thinks about us all the time. If God didn't give us no battles to fight, we wouldn't grow. Every now and then we have got fight some kind of battle, always remember God is on your side.

Paul's advice is to turn your worries into prayers, then pray more, if you worry, don't pray, if you pray, don't worry. Whenever you worry, stop and pray, don't worry about anything, instead of worrying about everything, pray about everything. Thank God for all he has done for you. He brought you last year, and He will bring you this year. He didn't bring us this far to leave us. He will never leave us, we are the ones that walk away and leave Him. Worrying paralyzes our prayer life when we get down don't, no what to do we should ask God for help. Worrying gets us nowhere, but prayer gets us in touch with the one who can handle all our problems (1Peter 4:16). Yet if any man suffers as a Christian let him not be ashamed, but let him glorify God on this behalf. It is not shameful to suffer for being a Christian. When Peter and John were persecuted for preaching the Good News, they rejoiced because of there persecution was a mark of God's approval of there work. This is what Jesus was telling us when He takes up their cross to follow Him.

Walk away from worrying, get away just you and Jesus, go into your praying place only you and Jesus deny yourself, get self out of the way, then Jesus said to take up your cross and follow me. The hardest thing for a person to do is to deny herself, get herself out of the picture. Jesus bore the hard part He carries the Big heavy Cross.

Jesus fought the batter by carrying the big heavy cross so our little cross would not be heavy. The Hem writer said must Jesus bear the cross alone, and all the world goes free, He went to say, No there's a cross for everyone and their across for me. The cross is a suffering Journal and a trouble journal, we will have struggles in this journal, Jesus had trouble with His journal. Every child of God hath his or her cross to bear, but in every cross, there is good in it.

You don't run after blessings, let the blessing run after you, God has promised an increase for those who praise Him from A SINCERE HEART. Even Jesus himself was not accepted as a prophet in his hometown. Many people have a similar attitude. Don't be surprised if your Christian life and faith are not easily understood or accepted by those who know you well. Because they know your background, your failures. And your defects, they may not see past those to the new person you have become. Let God work in your life, pray to be a positive witness for him, and be patient. Satan does not like to see no one change their life from serving him and come over to the LORD side, Satan always says, I remember when she or he did this or that they are not saved. Satan does not want you serving God. They do not want you save, once we are saved, Jesus says that he will put our sins as for as the east is from the west.

When you get away with Jesus in your prayer closet just you and Jesus, talk to Him, you can tell Jesus anything that you want to, and he wants to tell nobody. (Psalm 28:6) Blessed be the: LORD, because he hath heard the voice of my supplication There are no problems too big for Jesus The same power that raised Christ from the dead is available to help us with our daily problems. When you feel weak and limited, don't despair. Remember that God can give you strength. The power that controls the creation and raises Him from the dead is available to you. We often wish we could escape troubles, the pain grief, loss, sorrow, and failure, or even the small daily frustrations that continuously wear us down. God promises to be our source of power, courage, and wisdom, helping us through our problems. Sometimes he chooses to deliver us from those problems. When trouble strikes, don't get frustrated with God. Instead, humbly admit that you need God's help and thank him for being by your side. Get away just you and Jesus the gospel is not only what we believe but also what we must live. The Holy Spirit leads us in faithfulness, so we can avoid lust and fraud, live as though you expect Christ's return at any time. Don't be caught unprepared.

The Holy Spirit helps us to remain strong in faith, able to show genuine love to others and maintain our moral character even when we are being persecuted, slandered, or oppressed. When you get away just you and Jesus, and you don't know what to say, just say Jesus, Jesus, He will hear you because there is power in the name of Jesus James call the various trials we face he calls them the trying of our faith. He said he count it all joy, all things work together for Good. Our trail and our little tribulation strengthen us.

CHAPTER 10

Amazing Grace

(**E**phesians 2: 8) For by grace, you have been saved through FAITH and that not of yourselves, it is the gift of GOD.

For by grace, you have been saved through faith and that not of yourselves, saving grace is not of yourself it is the gift of God. Even faith is not of yourself; it too is the gift of God. Faith comes by hearing, and hearing by the Word of God. Without FAITH, there is no salvation.

Our sins may be great and many, but God's grace is greater, Christ settled the question of sin on the cross, we accepted Jesus as LORD and SAVIOR (1 John 3:2). Beloved now are we the sons of God, and it doth not yet appear what we shall be. But we know that when he shall appear, we shall be like him. For we shall see him as he is, we must never forget our past, the condition from which Jesus saved us. Those memories are the best fuel for our gratitude to Christ for all he has done on our behalf.

God could have left us spiritually dead, but he didn't, he did not save us because of. He keeps us in spite of what he saw in us. When I was a little girl, my Mother and Father learned all the children: For God so loved the world that he gave his only begotten son that whosoever believeth in him should not perish, but have everlasting life.

God paid dearly with the life of his son, he paid the highest price he could pay, Jesus accepted our punishment he paid the price for our sins. And then offered us the new life he had brought for us. Grace is the love of God shown to the unlovely, Grace id the peace of God given to the restless.

Grace is unconditional love toward a person who does not deserve it, nothing can be hidden from God, He knows about everyone, everywhere. Everything about you and I. He is seeing all we do, all we think, even when we are unaware of his presence he is right there. Also, when we try to hide from him, he sees all of us at once.

We can't have no secrets from God he knows all about us he still loves us, but what we do wrong is coming up again. Have you ever felt that God didn't hear your prayers, be sure you are praying with a willing spirit. Be ready to do what God wants, God responds to his obedient children. Prayer is our approach to God and us to come boldly unto the throne of grace.

Some Christians approach God with there heads hanging, afraid to ask him to meet their needs. When you come to the throne of grace, come bolding. He is our FATHER, OUR KING, OUR FRIEND, and OUR COUNSELOR. He is our everything. God loves us He loves us so much he sent his son Jesus to die for us so we can have eternal life through FAITH in Him. He broke the power of death with his resurrection.

We do not deserve to be saved, but God offers us salvation anyway, I thank God every day for offering us salvation. All we have to do is believe and accept his offer (Romans 10: 9) That if thou shalt confess with thy mouth the Lord Jesus, and shalt believe in thine heart that God hath raised His Son Jesus from the dead, thou shalt be saved. Meaning anyone denying the bodily resurrection of Jesus Christ cannot legitimately claim to be a Christian. He is still an unbeliever, for the death and resurrection of Christ is the central event in salvation.

When God forgives our sins, our record is wiped clean (Psalm 103:12). When we ask forgiveness, God will put our sins away from us as far as the east is from the west (Romans 4:25). Paul said that Jesus was delivered for our offenses and who was raised again for our justification. When you accept Jesus Christ as your savior, an exchange takes place. We give Christ our sins, and he forgives us and makes us right with God. You may be thinking my sins are too many, too big He won't forgive me. Paul had been the enemy of the Christian church, he was persecuting believers. He felt unworthy to be called an apostle a chosen messenger of Christ. When God, through with Paul, he was deeply humbled. Grace is God's voluntary and loving favor given to those he saved.

We can't earn it, nor do we deserve it. The songwriter made it so clear: Amazing grace how sweet the sound that saved a wretch like me. I once was lost, but now I'm found blind, but now I see. God used a thorn in Paul's flesh to teach him about grace. We do not know what Paul's thorn in the flesh was, he did not tell us what it was. But we all have some kind of thorn. We just like Paul, prayed for this thorn to be moved, God refused Paul was a very self-sufficient person this thorn was painful for him.

Three times Paul prayed for healing and did not receive it, God doesn't heal some believers of their physical ailments, we don't know why some are spared, and others aren't. But we will understand it better by-and-by.

God chooses according to his divine purposes, our task is to pray to believe, have faith, and to trust. When we are strong in abilities or resources, we are tempted to do God's work on our own that can lead to pride. When we are weak, we are allowing God to fill us with his power then we are stronger than we could ever be on our own.

Paul said there was given to him a thorn in the flesh, a messenger of Satan put it there, but he had to get approver from God. He prayed, prayed, and prayed. The Lord told him that my grace is sufficient for thee, my strength is made perfect in weakness (James 4: 6). But he giveth more grace. Wherefore he saith God resisteth the proud, but giveth grace unto the humble.

It should be impressed upon our hearts and minds how much God hates pride. Pride in our lives will cause God to turn from our prayers and withhold His presence and grace from us. To be exalted in our own minds and to seek honor and the esteem of others to satisfy our feelings of pride is to shut out the help of God. But for those who humbly submit themselves to God and draw near to Him, there is abundant grace, mercy, and help in every situation of life.

We must draw nigh to God. God promises to draw near to all those who turn from sin, purify their hearts, and call upon Him in true repentance. God's nearness will bring His presence, grace, blessing, and love.

He that lives in you is more significant than He that in the world, tell yourself I can do all things through Christ. God is anger for a moment, as soon as we repentance His passion is gone. He will forget, He will forgive, He loves us just that much. Aren't you glad that in the plans of God He came our way and brought us salvation? If it had not been for the Lord on our side, where would we be?

We have not been save all our lives, some of us been mass up from the toe up, at one time in somebody life you wanted to give up. (Psalm 30:5) For his anger endure but a moment in his favor is life weeping may endure for a night but joy cometh in the morning. The night does not last always, the day got to come. Trouble don't last forever. Our happiness is in God's favor if we have God favor we have enough. His support is the life of the soul. It is spiritual life; it is life eternal.

You thought there is no use of going on, no use to keep praying, God comes on his timing, not our, I don't know what you are going through, I do know that we all have some issues in our life. Don't you ever give up on God? Jesus suffered as we do that is why He can help us, He lived as a man, He went through all the sorrows and troubles of life, but he didn't give up.

There is a season for everything, Just keep the Faith, your

prayers are just delayed not denied. David prayed he prayed for mercy, have mercy upon me. He prayed for grace to help in time of need Lord be my helper. In due time God delivered him out of his troubles. His prayers were answered, and his mourning was turned into dancing. God will answer your prayers on his timing, and on his conditions, It is easy to be frightened by the wickedness we see all around us and to be overwhelmed by the problems we face. Evil is obviously much stronger than we are. (1 John 4 ch) assures us that God is stronger and that Jesus will conquer all evil, and his spirit and his word live in our hearts. (Ephesians 4:26) Be ye angry and sin not let not the sun go down upon your wrath.

Grace helps us with our angry, the Bible doesn't tell us that we shouldn't feel mad, but it points out that it is important to handle our anger correctly, deal with our anger immediately in a way that builds relationships, rather than destroying them. If we nurse our anger, we will allow Satan to divide us. Don't let the sun go down on your passion with someone or with you hating someone.

Nothing sinful or evil can exist in God's presence (1 Peter 2:24) who his own self bare our sins in his own body on the tree. That we were being dead to sins should live unto righteousness by whose stripes ye were healed. Christ died for our sins in our place, so we would not have to suffer the punishment we deserve (1 John 4:12). Tell us that no man hath seen God at any time, if we love one another God dwelleth in us, and his love is perfected in us. No one has seen God, how can we ever know him? When we love one another, God reveals himself to others through us, and his love is made complete.

When we become Christians we receive the Holy Spirit, God's presence in our life is a proof that we really belong to him (1 John 4: 19) We love Him because he first love us Vs. 20 If a man says, I love God and hateth his brother of his sister. He is a liar for he that loveth not his brother whom he hath seen. How can he love God, whom he hath not seem?

A Christian should do what Christ tells them to do, live as Christ wants us to live, what does Christ ask us to do? Believe on the name of his SON JESUS CHRIST, and love one another.

(1 John 4:20) If a man says I love God and hateth his brother, he is a liar. He that loveth not his brother whom he hath seen, How can he love God whom he hath not seem. It is easy to say we love God when it doesn't cost us anything more than weekly attendance at religious service.

The real test of our love for God is how we treat the people right in front of us, our family members, other believers that we go to church with. We cannot truly love God while neglecting to love those who are created in his image.

CHAPTER 11

Speak to Your Mountain

The kind of prayer that moves mountains is a prayer for the fruitfulness of God's kingdom. It seems impossible to move a mountain into the sea. (Mark 11: 23). So Jesus used that picture to show that God can do anything, God will answer your prayers, but on his timing on his conditions, we must believe. We must not hold a grudge against another person, we must not pray with selfish motives our request must be for the good of his kingdom.

To pray effectively, we need FAITH in God, not faith in the object of our request. Jesus said all things are possible unto thee, it's not what I will but what thou will. Jesus prayed with God's interest in mind when we pray, we can express our desires, but we should want his will above ours.

Jesus said whosoever shall say unto this mountain, Be thou removed and be thou cast into the sea, he shall have whatsoever he saith (Mark 11: 23). Jesus is telling people to confess God's Word, and to speak to the mountains in our lives. What to do about those mountains, he said we are supposed to talk to them.

What do I speak we speak God's Word to those mountains so we can go on and possess everything God has for us in this life. What mountain stands between you and possessing everything God has for you in life.

Maybe your mountains is a financial need, perhaps sickness,

or confusion, many believers have trouble with self-pity. They always have pity parties. Self-pity, the poor-ole me attitude leads to depression and frustration. It doesn't matter what problems you face in life, Jesus Christ has already triumphed over them (Matthew 17:20). Jesus said because of your unbelief verily I say unto you if ye have faith as a grain of mustard seed ye shall say unto this mountain remove hence to yonder place, and it shall remove, and nothing shall be impossible unto you.

Jesus was showing his disciples how important faith would be to them if you are facing a problem that seems as big and immovable as a mountain. Jesus said to turn your eyes from the mountain and look to Him. Then you will be able to overcome the obstacles that stand in your way.

(Hebrews 11: 6) Without FAITH, it is impossible to please Him, For he that cometh to God must believe that he is and that he is a rewarder of them that diligently seek him. God assures us that all who honestly ask him will be rewarded. Faith cometh by hearing and hearing by the Word of God.

God will never forsake those who trust in him, his promise does not mean we would not have trials and tribulations. It means God himself will never leave us no matter what we face. If God gave us no rough roads to walk, no mountains to climb, and no battle to fight, we would not grow. We often wish we could escape trouble. The pains of grief, loss, sorrow, and the failure or even the small daily frustration that continuously wear us down, God promises to be our source of power

It might be seen sometime that God did not hear our prayers, God hears every prayer, but HE answers according to his wisdom. In our deepest sorrow, God cares He reminded us how much he understands us. He knows even the number of hairs on our head, so offer we waver between faith and fear. Sometimes we feel so discouraged seen like no one care, no one understands, all ways remember that Jesus cares. He knows all our problem, and see every tear that falls from our eyes.

God wants to carry our burdens, but so often we continue to bear them ourselves even when we say we are trusting in Jesus. Jesus is our shelter when we are afraid, He protects us, He carries us through all the dangers and fears of life we have to trust him. Have Faith in him, (Psalm 91:1) Tell us he that dwelleth in the secret place of the higher shall abide under the shadow of the Almighty.

Sometimes God allowed trouble to come, he allowed problems to go to the Israelites to help them. Our pain can be helpful because they humble us, we pray more, it makes us dependent upon God, make us more compassionate toward others that are going through troubles.

You remember Job's most crucial test was not the pain and suffering, he did not understand while it happened our most crucial test may be that we must trust God's goodness even though we don't know why our lives are going a certain way. We have got to learn how to speak to our mountains. But we need to realize that when we go out and start moving the mountains in our life. It's a big job, mountains don't always get moved overnight sometimes it takes time, it takes prayers to move those things out of our way that has been there for so long.

(Luke 5: 18) Tells us that some men brought in a bed, a man paralyzed laid on it. They couldn't find no way to get him in the house. The house was packed out couldn't get him in the door or push him through the window. They wanted to lay him before Jesus and when they couldn't find no way to get in the house because of the great multitude they had a mountain to move, and they didn't let nobody stop them.

The Bible tells us that they went upon the housetop. When Jesus saw their faith, he said unto them, your sins are forgiven. It wasn't the sick man's faith that impressed Jesus but the trust of his friends.

So many times we move before God tells us to move stand still waiting on God's timing, we must trust God to give us patience during those difficult times. We want other people to like us, and sometime we will do almost anything to win their approval. But God tells us to put out energy into pleasing him. He is our best friend, He loves us. Folks can find an excuse for doing almost anything, God looks behind that excuse to the motives of the heart. When we communicate with God, we don't demand what we want. We discuss with him Lord what you want for me.

God is the source of our love, he loved us enough to sacrifice his Son. Jesus is our example of what it means to love. When we pray and move the mountain whatever in the way, then the Holy Spirit gives us the power to love in our hearts and makes us more and more like Jesus.

Sometimes we have a difficult time forgiving someone who wrongs us, imagine how hard it would be to forgive all people no matter what they had done. This is what God has done in Jesus. No matter what sin has been committed all we have to do is turn from sin receive Jesus Christ forgiveness and commit your heart to him, he loves us, he is our best friend, when you do that, the mountain in your life got to go.

Jesus is the bright and morning star, He is a friend that will stick closer than a brother. I heard my old grandmamma in her lifetime. Baby, he is a bridge over troubled waters, shielded in the time of a storm, he is bread in a stoving land, My mama said one day we will live with Him, he is a Dr when you are on your sick bed. I heard someone else say he is a burden bearer, the light of the world, he is our everything.

Paul, he and Silas, were put in the Philippian Jail they laid many stripes on them, and cast them into prison we didn't commit no crime. We kept the faith, we believe that God would make away for us. They started to have a prayer meeting at midnight Paul and Silas had to pray they were moving mountains out of there way

Jesus mission would involve great pain. Suffering, disappointment, and grief because of the sins of humankind, all those who follow Jesus will experience a measure of suffering and distress. Jesus endures punishment so that we may be delivered from our diseases and sicknesses, as well as from our sins. It is right and good for us to pray for physical healing that we may be delivered from our disease and sicknesses, as well as from our sins he takes the illness and grief that belong to us, lift them upon himself. But he took it and paid the penalty for our sins, the sentence of death, we can be forgiven and have peace with God (Romans 5:3).

And not only so, but we glory in tribulations also knowing that tribulation worketh patience. The word tribulation refers to all kinds of trials that may press in upon us. This includes such things as a financial or physical need, trying circumstances the pressure of sorrow, sickness, persecution, mistreatment.

Some people have problems when it comes to forgiving people, they are hurting themselves. The key to forgiving others is remembering how much Jesus has forgiven us. I know it is difficult for you to forgive someone who has wrong you pray to ask God to move that mountain out of your way, God love can help you love and forgive others, that is one way you know you are saved. Don't try to get even with people that have wrong you, pray for them and let God fight the battle.

God promises to reward our faith by giving us his power and helping us bear persecution. Suffering for our faith will strengthen us to serve Christ. We must be faithful to him. We should not be afraid when we see an evil increase. God is in control, no matter how evil the world becomes. God guards us during Satan's attacks. We can have victory over evil by remaining faithful to God.

CHAPTER 12

Run the Race with Patience

(H)ebrews 12:1-13) I Press toward the mark for the prize of the high calling of God in Christ Jesus. Our gold should be to know Jesus Christ better and better And to be like him. And to be all Jesus had in mind for us, we should not let anything take our eyes off our goal, which is Jesus Christ.

Paul tells us in (Philippians 4: 12) That he knew both how to be abased, and I know how to abound. Everywhere and in all things, I am instructed both to be full and to be hungry both to abound and to suffer need. Vs. 13, Then I can do all things through Christ which strengthens me. So like Paul, we can learn to be content in any situation we face. Paul knows how to be content, whether he had much or little.

We need to learn to rely on God's promises and Christ Power to help you be content. He will supply our every need, not our every want (Hebrews 12:1). Wherefore seeing we also compassed about with so great a cloud of witnesses, let us lay aside every weight and the sin which doth so easily beset us and let us run with patience the race that is set before us.

Paul is telling us to have faith like the great Heroes. By FAITH was translated that he should not see death.

By FAITH Noah being warned of God of things not seen as yet,

By FAITH, Abraham was called to go out into a place which he should after receive for an inheritance.

By FAITH, Sara conceives a child.

By FAITH Moses when he was born, He hid three months of his parents.

Let us lay aside every weight and the sin which doth so easily beset us, and let us run with patience the race that is set before us. We do not struggle alone, and we are not the first to struggle with the problems we face. Others have run the race and won. Long distance runners work hard to build endurance and strength with God's help, we can do more than we think (Hebrews 2:9). But we see Jesus who was made a little lower than the angels for the suffering of death,

Crowned with glory and an hour that he by the grace of God should taste death for every man, God's kindness to us led Christ to his death, Christ suffers and die so that we could have eternal life. Jesus suffering made him a perfect leader. He did not suffer for his own salvation, but in obeying, he became the complete perfect sacrifice for us.

The Christian life involves hard work, it requires us to give up whatever endangers our relationship with God. God wants us to run with endurance, we struggle against sin with the power of the Holy Spirit.

We must keep our eyes on Jesus, we stumble when we look away from him to stare at other things. To run the race that God has set before us, we must lay aside the excess weight that slows us down. Always choose friends who also committed to the race.

Much of our weight may result from the crowd you run with (Psalm26:5). David said I have hated the congregation of evildoers and will not sit with the wicked. Should we stay away from unbelievers? NO Jesus demonstrated that we must go among unbelievers to help them. There is a difference between being with unbelievers and being one of them. Don't let unbelievers harms your witness for God. (2 Corinthians 6:14).

Be ye not unequally yoked together with unbelievers for what fellowship hath righteousness with unrighteousness and what communion mix light with darkness.

(Proverb 11:12) When says my sons despise not the chastening of the Lord neither be weary of his correction for whom the Lord loveth he correcteth even as a father the son in whom he delighteth. (James 1:2-3) James said don't lose your courage and give up when you are corrected or disciplined by God. (Hebrews 12:6) The Lord corrects disciplines and teaches by trail by affliction and by tribulation everyone whom he loves.

The Lord had only one SON without sin. He has none without suffering. (1 Peter 1:6-7) The best we try to live we are like files RAPES. No trial or suffering is pleasant, nor does it bring joy at the time, it is difficult and painful, that is the reason while we have to run this race with patience. Run and don't look back, and don't give up. The Christian life was never promised to be an easy life to live. Don't get discouraged and give up, keep the faith, God just wants to hear from you. Make sure you have on God full armor, pray and keep the FAITH. Put on all God's armor, pray on all occasions. Endure suffering like a soldier, don't get tied up in worldly affairs. Run this race with patience, don't give in to the Devil running for everlasting life. Remember that the BATTLE is not given to the swift nor to the strong. It is given to the ones that hold out until the end.

In this race of faith, we look to Jesus as our example of trust in God, Run, and don't give up, the Christian life was never promised to be an easy life to live. Don't get discouraged and give up do good to everyone. Put on all of God's armor, pray on all occasions, endure suffering like a soldier, don't get up in worldly affairs, Run the Race with patience, run the Race with patience, run because for everlasting life.

Let me illustrate the principle that if one fails to exercise self-denial for the sake of others. renounces his rights out of thoughtful consideration for the conviction of others. The "prize," the "incorruption" crown is the victory of gaining eternal salvation, the precious goal of the Christian life. This goal can only be won by giving up some of our rights for the sake of others and by renouncing those things that would take us out of the race altogether.

We should live by grace; this means trusting entirely in Jesus and his power Every day, He desires to guide you and help you with your daily problems. Those who have work to do for God must stir up themselves to do it and strengthen themselves for it, being active in the grace that is in Christ. (Psalm 13:5) But I have trusted in thy mercy my heart shall rejoice in thy salvation.

David expressed his feelings to God and found strength by the end of his prayer, he was able to profess hope and trust in God. Through prayer, we can express our feelings and talk about our problems out with God. Out emotions are not controlled by the events around us, but by faith in God's ability to give you strength. When nothing makes sense, and when troubles seem more than you can bear, remember that God gives power. Take your eyes off your difficulties and look to God.

We are God people we need to live in the strength of his Spirit, have confidence that one day there will be victory over evil. We can be assured that he is God and will do what is right in this confusing world. Trust God, even when we don't understand why events occur as they do.

God was and is the ruler over the hold world; sometimes he seems so far off (Psalm 44: 23&24) David said he appeared to be asleep. The disciples wondered why Jesus was sleeping when they needed his help during the storm. He was building their faith, all they had to do was call him. David was faithful to God and trusted wholeheartedly in him. But he felt the pressure of his problems as much as anyone.

Instead of giving up or giving in, he held on to his FAITH and waited with the patient. In times of trials, it is much harder to hold on. Trust in God mercy it will anchor you in any storm, run this race with the patient. Whatever come your way, trust God, He will take care of you.

When God does not answer immediately keep on trusting him to keep running the race, don't stop and give up. He said I want to forsake you and I won't leave you Some times He will leave us in our little storm to strength us build up our faith and teach us how to wait on the patient.

Lord, I'm pressing on I need strength I need more knowledge give us more love, and Lord, please help me with attitude, Jesus helps me to be what you want me to be I am pressing on I got to go home with Jesus when he comes. Got to hear him say well done.

Sometime our way will get dark but keep pressing, you might get tired don't get discouraged never give up on Jesus. Press your way some time don't feel good in the body but keep pressing God will see you through.

Paul said be encourage no matter how difficult the fight seem, keep fighting.

CHAPTER 13

Ride out your Storm

A child of God can lay down at night with so many burdens, lay down worrying how are we going to make it, but when morning comes, it's all working out. The redeemed praise the Lord for deliverance from dangerous situations. Sometimes we forget to give God thanks until we are going through trials and tribulations then we cry out to the Lord.

(Psalm 107:29) Exhorts the redeemed to praise the Lord for deliverance from danger situations. All believers who are in affliction cry out to the Lord, it builds up your faith and encourages us during those times when we need God to intervene specifically in our lives.

When Israel was wandering in the wilderness four times in this Psalms God delivered them out of their distresses. Many times God will bring his children to a place where their own self-sufficiency fails, and where no human being can help so that they might cry out to Him in humble and childlike faith.

We all are going through some kind storm and if you have not been in a storm, can I tell you just to wait awhile. God promises to carry us through all our storms, nobody likes storms they always tear up and hurt. David said O that I had wings like a dove, for then would I fly away and be at rest. David was close to

God, but he had moments when he wanted to get away from it all. He tried to escape the storms of life.

When the winds become stormy in your life, just truth God. He brought you through last year, and He will bring you through every time if you keep the faith and trust him. Sometimes it is hard, I been there being reel from side to side. God will calm the storm just ride it out.

When we go through the storms of life, it's good to cry out to the Lord. That when we learn to pray, be patient have faith trust, and believe. When we are going through, we want somebody to carry our weight, bear our pains, and carry our burdens. The only man I know who can carry other weight, depression, and loads are Jesus.

Many time when we are going through the storm of life, we will set around feeling sorry for our self. Stop feeling sorry for yourself, stop waiting for someone to pat you on the back. Stop sitting around, waiting for someone to encourage you. GREATER is He that lives in you than he that lives in the world. Waiting on somebody to come lay hands on you. If Jesus lives in our heart, we have enough power in our hands to heal our self

(John 14:16) And I will pray for the Father, and he shall give you another Comforter, that he abide with you forever; Jesus will pray that the Father will provide the Comforter only to those who are serious about their love for Him and their devotion to His Word,

Jesus tells us in his word: If you abide in me and my words abide in you, you will ask what you festive, and it shall be done for you. In this troubled world, you learn to encourage yourself, setting around with low-self esteem, we have a heavenly Father who can do all things.

Jesus entered into a ship, and his disciples followed him there was a great storm in the sea; the boat was covered with the waves. Jesus was tired and sleeping, see Jesus could sleep in a storm. I get a little nervous during storms, and so were the disciples. Jesus was tied and sleeping, Jesus could sleep in a storm. I am a bit worried during storms, and so were the disciples.

When the storm of life comes, and we are toss from side to side. The disciples went to Jesus woke Him up, saying Lord wake up and save us, if you don't wake up we will die. All they had to do was ride out the storm. They had the master of all storm on board. Jesus asks while are you so fearful? Where is your FAITH in God? He got up, rebuked the winds and the sea.

The disciples began to talk among themselves, who is this man? Even the winds and the sea obey him (Psalm 107: 26-35). When there a storm of life in your home just remember He maketh the storm a calm so that the waves thereof are still (Matthew 8:26). And he saith unto them, Why are ye fearful, O ye of little faith.

When Jesus returned to the other side of the sea of Galilee, there was a crowd of people waiting on him. Jairus comes to get Jesus to heal his little girl not to raise her from the dead his faith was small. He believes Jesus could raise her up off the sick bed, but not from the dead. While Jesus was on his way to Jairus house, he had to stop for another emergency. There was a woman that had been riding out her storm for eight long years (Luke 13:10) said that Jesus was teaching in one of the synagogues on the Sabbath. There was a woman who had a spirit of infirmity for eighteen long years. here is another lady was bowed together, and could not lift up herself, when Jesus saw her he called her to him and said to the her "woman thou art loosed from thine in

He laid hands on her and immediately, and she was made straight and glorified God. I have had many problems in my life. There of times I felt like I am broken if it not one thing, it is another that's life, but I learn how to ride my storm out. Just like this woman, your miracles are coming out of broken pieces. Sometimes, we have to mix faith and patents together and wait on Jesus. God does not move on your time, He moves on his time.

This woman had been bent for 18 years, this woman didn't give up. She rode her storm out. The storm is not easy to ride out, any time God is teaching you how to keep the FAITH, Trust, believe, and how to stay humble with a sincere heart. Sin affects our minds and heart just as a shepherd is concerned enough about one lost sheep to go search the hill. God is concerned about every human being he creates he is not willing that any should perish.

When we trust God, we walk with him, we grow in grace he carries our burdens, he carries our sins, our shame. Sometimes when we go through trials, it is not for us, it for someone else, to get there soul right with God. Sometimes God uses people to help us grow. We can enter directly into God's presence through prayer, God will welcome you with open arms because we are his children.

Someone might say I been praying for a long time and he has not answered me. Where is your faith? He did not say he would come at every call, keep the faith and wait. So many times while we are waiting, that old Devil will put another block in your way. Keep the faith and ride out your storm. But every now and then Storms will come in your life, hold on to your faith.

When caught in the storms of life, it is so easy to think God has lost control. God is always in control, just Ride out your storm. Sometimes you have to press your way, holding back the tears. Just like Jesus calmed the waves, he can calm whatever storms you and I face.

As they sailed, Jesus fell asleep, and there came down a storm of wind on the lake. The boat was filled with water, and they were in jeopardy, and they awoke Jesus and said, Master, we perish. Life storms will be like that sometime. Jesus arose and rebuked the wind and the raging water they ceased, and everything was calm. With little warning storm in our life can come up so quiet, just like the disciples were caught without warning, with short warning storms in our life can come up so quit. The disciples were caught without warning.

You can go to bed at night sleep great, get up the next morning have your coffee, and by noon you are so sad because a storm wind blowing in your house. Jesus controls storms of nature, and he manages our troubled heart. Sometimes on this road, we fall, get up, ask God to forgive you. We don't plan to fall, but sometimes we trip, (Micah 7:8). He says when I fall, he didn't say if I fall, but when I fall, I shall arise. Do you ever get down in the dumps you feel that everything you have dreamed about, everything you have waited for everything you planned for, Everything you have lived for just going down the drain because of the enemy? You wonder when will the storm end. Sometimes seen like you just want to throw up your hands and just quit. God is teaching you how to wait, be steadfastly unmoveable how to have faith and wait on him. And sometime God will not stop the storms, he will step on board and ride it out with you.

God gives us his Holy Spirit to help us obey and to provide us with the power to overcome sin. The power of God isn't activated by just the incidental touch, I'm sure that day a lot of people reached through the crowd and touched Jesus out of curiosity just to see if anything would happen. The power of God isn't activated by the unique touch you have got to stir up your faith. Before you reach out of him, you had better stir up your faith. I am so broken I just need a miracle in my life the wonders are coming out of the fractured pieces our your life.

Sometimes you have to mix Faith and patents together and wait. But do not set around feeling sorry for yourself waiting for someone to pat you on the back, need someone to carry your burdens. The only man I know who can take our weight, pains, and troubles are Jesus. Many times when we are going through the storms of life don't set around, feeling sorry for yourself.

The Bible tells us that this woman had an issue of blood for twelve long years, twelve years riding out her storm. The bible didn't give her name so you or I could put our name there, she had a problem why all the other women were having a good time enjoying life.

What I like about this woman she didn't give up she kept pressing her way, she kept on riding out her storm, sick, and weak as she was, but she did not give up. God is with us through every situation, in every trial he is protecting us loving us, guiding us, and he orders our steps. God is aware of everything that happens even to the little sparrows, we are far more valuable to him than sparrows are. We are so glad that God sent his only Son to die for us.

God places so much value on you, and I should never fear personal threats or difficult trials. This doesn't mean that God will take away all our trouble (Matthew 10:16). Jesus said, behold I send you forth as sheep among wolves, be ye, therefore, wise as serpents and harmless as doves. You are a child of God, so you look to Jesus for your protection.

The real test is your FAITH, see if you can stand up for Christ in spite of your troubles (Proverbs 1:7). The FEAR of the Lord is the beginning of knowledge. But fools despise wisdom and instruction. The first step to enlightenment is the fear of the Lord. Faith in God should be the foundation of your understanding of the world, our attitude, and our actions. Trust God, he will make you wise.

We wish we could escape troubles, the pains of grief, the lost the sorrow and the failure, even the daily frustrations that always wear you down, but we can't we have to go through. God promises to carry us through, he promises to be with us, He promises never to leave you. In this life, if it's not one thing, it's another. The storms of life come so many times and so many ways. When we are not looking, it occurs when we are not thinking, everything is going fine get up in the morning feeling good, but by night up pop the storm.

Many times we try to take the storm in our hands. Winds are life is no match for you and I. We can weather no storm. There is a beautiful old hymn that says: He gives us peace in the middle of the storm. We don't know how to deal with winds, we are like the disciples. When the wind blows in our house, in our family, we get afraid (Isaiah 41:10). Tell us to fear not for I am with you, be not dismayed for I am your God. I will strengthen you, I will help you. I will uphold you with my righteous right hand.

In the Strom of life, we always say I got, it's under control, there will be a storm in our life sometimes we can pray Jesus will come to that storm. And sometime, Jesus will step on broad with us and ride the storm out (Matthew 14:27-31). One thing that holds my attention in this amazing story: Is the figure of Jesus walking on water. Right here in this passage of scripture is really challenging us to rise to a new level, another level so that we will be able to see what his power is all about.

We have read about it, we have heard it preach about many times. We have been through many storms. Trouble is all around them; it's dark; it's about 3:00 a.m. in the morning. These disciples are wrestling with this storm. The only authority that they have one this storm is a voice of fear.

The Devil smells fear, when He can find a little FEAR he will come in work with your mind God has given us love and a sound mind, The disciples were in the middle of a storm in the middle of the storm. The only thing they could think of: If Jesus were here, he would know how to handle a storm. They were so full of fear, the disciples saw Jesus walking on water.

Jesus knew his disciples just like he know us, one of his disciples said, look it's a ghost. In the middle of a storm of your storm. Peter said if it is you bid me come to you, Jesus said come Peter got out of the boat walking on water, everything until he took his eyes off Jesus. We may not walk on water, but we walk through tough situations.

Keep your eye on Jesus, which is his word, Keep the faith truth him, keep faith during your storm. Hold on Ride out your Strom. If you hold on, God will show up in your storm. He does not come on your timing but on his schedule.

He will show up when you think you just can't take any more, He will show up to wipe the tears from your eyes. The storms of life get hard sometimes. God is speaking all over the world, telling men and women to turn from sin. He is telling people to come unto me all ye that labor and heavy laden and I will give you rest. Take my yoke upon you and learn of me. I am meek and lowly in heart, and you shall find rest unto your souls. Jesus tells us that his yoke is easy, and my burden is light.

Jesus' gracious invitation comes to all "that labor and are heavy laden" with the troubles of life and the sins of their own human nation. By coming to Jesus, becoming His savant, and obeying His direction, Jesus will free you from your insurmountable burdens and give you rest, peace, and His Holy Spirit to lead you through life. What trials and cares you will be borne with His help and grace.

(Mark 5: 25-27) And a certain woman, which had an issue of blood twelve years, and had suffered many things of many physicians, and had spent all that she had, and was nothing bettered, but rather grew worse, When she had heard of Jesus, came in the press behind, and touched his garment.

This woman had a problem while other women were having a good time enjoying life. Sometimes we feel our problems will keep us from God. But he is always ready to help, no matter how impossible the problem seems to us. We should never allow our fear to keep us from approaching him. It was the contact and presence of Jesus that mattered His touch has healing power because He sympathizes with our infirmities is the source of life and grace. Our responsibility in seeking healing is to draw near to Jesus and to abide in His presence. Stir up your Faith and ride out your storm.

CHAPTER 14

No Cross No Crown

God promises to carry us through, He promises to be with us, He promises not to leave us. No Cross No Crown, Sometimes it takes trials to keep us on our knees. Everybody wants a crown, but nobody wants a cross. Jesus used this picture of his followers, taking up their crossed to follow Him. Following Jesus mean a real commitment no turning back.

To take up our cross and follow Jesus means to be willing to publicly identify with him, be prepared to face even suffering and death for his sake, Jesus. Jesus said and he that taketh not his cross and followeth after me is not worthy of me. How much we love God can be measured by how well we treat others.

If we cannot bear our little cross and come after him, we cannot be his disciple (Luke 9: 23). If any man comes after me, let him deny himself, and take up his cross daily and follow me. We are committed daily to follow Jesus that choice determines our eternal destiny. The cross of Christ is a symbol of suffering, death, shame, and rejection. When we as believers take up our cross and follow Christ, we deny our own selves

We suffer in a lifelong battle against sin, the highest glory and privilege of any believer is to suffer for Christ and the gospel, Christians must be willing to suffer to share in the sufferings of Christ and the gospel. Christians must be willing to suffer to share in the sufferings of Christ.

(Acts 9:16) For 'I will show him how great things he must suffer for my name's sake. Faith in Christ brings great blessings but often great suffering, too. God calls us to commitment, not to comfort. He promises to be with us through pain and hardship, not to spare us from them.

Jesus tells us in (Luke 14:27) whosoever doth not bear his cross and come after me cannot be my disciples. Following Jesus means total submission to Him. No man having put his hand to the plow and looking back is fit for the kingdom of God. (Exodus 20:5). Thou shalt not bow down thyself to them, nor serve them: for I the Lord thy God am a jealous God.

If they didn't learn that the God who led them out of Egypt was the only true God, they could not be his people no matter how faithfully they kept the other nine commandments thus. God made this his first commandment. Today we allow specific values to become gods to us. Money, fame, or pleasure can become gods when we concentrate too much on them for meaning and security.

Jesus wants total dedication, not halfhearted commitment, we have to accept the cross along with the crown. God desires to make us perfect and complete, not to keep us from all pain instead of complaining about our struggles. We should see them as opportunities for growth. I heard a story years ago about the cross. This man kept talking about his cross was too heavy he was tired of carrying it, every day the same cross he got tired of pulling it. Jesus told him to take it to the warehouse, put it up, and pick you out another cross. The man walked and look, he walks, and he walks. Then he saw one a little cross, he said I'll take this little one. Jesus told him you looked, and you walked, but that is the same cross you had in the beginning. No cross, No crown.

(Romans 4:25) Paul talks like he was delivered for our

offenses. And raised again for our justification, when we accept Jesus Christ as our savior an exchange takes place. We give Jesus Christ our sins, and he forgives us and makes us right with God. God is no respecter of person, what he has done for me, He will do for you. It all depends on our obedience and for us to follow Him completely. No Cross No Crown, God will never forsake those who trust in him,

His promise does not mean we would not have trials and tribulations, it means that God himself will never leave us. No matter what we face to get our crown, we have got to bear our cross. If God didn't give us rough roads to walk, somebody wouldn't pray. If he did give us no battle to fight, somebody wouldn't grow.

I wish we could escape troubles, pains, we have got deny self, get out of the way then Jesus said to take up your cross and follow me. You remember the Hem writer said must Jesus bear the cross alone, and all the world go free, No there's a cross.

For everyone and there is a cross. When you are suffering you are not by yourself, Jesus is right by your side He loves us so much.

He got into the RED SEA one day, He got into the BIG FISH, He got into the LIONS DENS, He got into the FIRE FURNACES, He got into The JAIL CELLS made it real and rock. When going through the storm of life, God is right there. The heavy cross He carried was for you and me.

Paul said there was given to him a thorn in the flesh, a messenger of Satan got approver from God. Paul said I prayed, and I prayed, and I prayed, No Cross, No Crown. God permits Satan to destroy all Job's children, everything he had worked so hard for, his health, God called Job his servant. God's servants are faithful to him in all they do. They serve him with their whole lives. He was a model of trust and obedience to God, therefore, permitted Satan to attack him in an unusually harsh manner. Although God loves us, belief and obeying him does not shelter us from life's calamities. Setbacks, tragedies, and sorrows strike Christians and non-Christians alike. But in our trials, God expects us to express our Faith to the world. How do you respond to your troubles? Do you ask God, "Why me?" or do you say, "Use me, Lord Jesus"?

(Job 1:9) Satan attacked Job's motives, saying he was righteous only because he had no reason to turn against God. Ever since he had started following God, everything had gone well for him. Satan wanted to prove that Job worshiped God, not out of love, but because God had given him much.

Satan accurately why many people trust God. They are fair-weather believers, following God only when everything is going well or for what they can get. Adversity destroys this superficial Faith. But adversity strengthens real Faith by causing believers to dig their roots deeper into God to withstand the storms. How deep does your Faith go? Put the roots of your Faith down deep into God so that you can withstand any wind you may face.

When Jesus took Peter, James, and John with Him to the Garden, Gethsemane told them to sit here, watch for me while I go pray. Jesus went a few steps fell on his face cry out, O my Father if it is possible to let this pass from me nevertheless not as I will, but as thou wilt, He prayed the same Prayer two times. He went back to Peter, James, and John. Why could you not watch with me one hour? The Spirit is willing, but the flesh is weak.

The 3rd time he prayed O my Father if this cup may not pass away from me except I drink it, Thy will be done. No cross no crown, God knows when his children need help. He knows when the load gets too heavy, He knows when the road gets too rough, He sees you day by day toiling, sometimes with tears in your eyes. No Cross, No Crown.

Before Satan can do anything to us, he has to get a mission from God, at first God said he did not want Job harmed physically, but then he decided to allow it. Satan is unable to persuade God to go against his character: God is entirely and eternally good.

But God was willing to go along with Satan's plan because God knew the eventual outcome of Job's story, God cannot be fooled by Satan. Job's suffering was a test for him, just remember the prize is not given to the swift nor to the strong, but to the One that holds out to the end. Just think to yourself if I die right now, what would happen to my soul.

Every morning is a new morning, every day is a new day, every evening is a new evening, every night is a new night, someone is saying I have lots of time to get saved. Not knowing that God can come to get you any second. Paul said, encourage yourself. Don't get tired, don't get discouraged, don't give up. Press your way sometimes you don't feel good in the body

He said be encourage no matter how difficult the fight seem to keep fighting. The Lamb of God died as the final sacrifice for all sins, to pay the penalty for sin a life had to be given. God chose to Provide the sacrifice himself, this is the way our sins are forgiving, Jesus paid the price for your sins and mine.

Many people believe that to survive in the world, a person must be tough to be strong. But God says not by might nor by power but by the Spirit when we live for God, we cannot trust in our own strength or our abilities instead depend on God and work in the power of his Spirit.

(Revelation 5:6)The horns symbolize strength and power, All power is in Him. The eyes are equated with the seven lambs and the one spirit, he sees everybody at the same time. What a mighty God we serve, many people believe that to survive in this world, a person must be tough and strong.

Every creature in heaven the earth the sea and in the ground joins in the excellent chorus singing in that heavenly choir. You might say the life that I have lived I will never sing in the heavenly choir. People can feel so guilt-ridden by their past that they think God could never forgive and accept them. But consider Paul's history. He had scoffed at the teachings of Jesus, hunting down and murdering God's people before coming to Faith in Christ.

Remember God, forgave Paul and used him in his Kingdom to teach others. He also can forgive and use you, and we all have sinned and come short of the glory of God. Thank God for loving us so much, he sent his Son Jesus to die for us so we can get forgiveness for our sins just like Paul. The Christian life involves hard work. It requires us to give up whatever endangers our relationship with God, to run with endurance, and to struggle against sin with the power of the Holy Spirit. To live effectively, we must keep our eyes on Jesus. We stumble when we look away from him to stare at ourselves or at the circumstances surrounding us. We are running for Christ, not ourselves, and we must always keep him in sight.

James doesn't say if we face trials, but when we meet them. He assumes we will have trials and that it is possible to profit from them. We are not required to pretend to be happy when we face pain, but to have a positive outlook because of the results trials will bring. James tells us to turn our heard ships into times of learning. Tough times can teach us Patience.

CHAPTER 15

Them Praying Saints

God is so good to us; some people do not realize just how good he is. He wakes us up every morning, right on time He didn't let us sleep too late, He able you and I to wake up put on clothes. You do not wake up every morning by a clock when you thank about how good the Lord is to you. I can't hold my peace. It is praying time.

Even though our battle, and our trials, God is still good when we don't understand, He is always right by our side I remember when I was about 10 years old, my Grandmother would take young children and myself to the sanctified church that what we called it. One night my Grandmother had all of us on the auto crying Jesus, Jesus, Jesus, we had called Jesus so long until I just fall out, I thought if I fall out, so Grandmother will leave me along. She didn't she fall down on her knees, I remember her saying call Jesus, call him, I fall out to keep from calling him I was so tired out. Thank God for my breakthrough and thank God for my Grandmother back in those days, they would put a sheet over you. I fall down on the floor because I was tried my Grandmother fall down because she knew that I was just about to get my breakthrough. It was so Awesome, the rest of the children wanted to know how did I feel? It was a feeling that I had never felt before. They wanted to know while we don't feel like you, You have to work and get him for your self no one can give Him to you.

The next Sunday, I went to church, the preacher was preaching all at once the Holy Spirit touch me. The doors were closed, but a heavy wind came through the doors, and knot me off my seat. Every Sunday I would go church, but now I didn't want to go all my friends would ask me what was wrong with me, they thought I was losing my mind I can't tell you, you have got to know Him for yourself. They would say to me we thank you are losing your mind.

I cried to mama, telling her I didn't want to go back to church, my friend was picking on me. They are telling me that I have lost my mind. Mama told me you have not lost your mind, God is doing something in your life. I don't know what, tell your friends they better try to get what you have, but I am waiting and praying to see how God wants to use you. Every night I would go down on my knees praying to God. Fifteen years after all that happen, I'm still praying to ask God to show me the way. I knew that he lives in my heart, I felt that He wanted me to do something else. Two years later, I start every night. I would dream the same dream that I was preaching God Word, and the Subject was Let God Be the Judge. Two many people were pointing fingers at me, telling me what God didn't do. See by now, I know what God can do. I knew that he was calling me out to preach his word, I couldn't go until God said go. The Devil tried to stop me, I told that Devil that God is the Judge. And God is in charge

(Ephesians 6:18-19) Praying always with all Prayer and supplication in the Spirit and watching thereunto with all perseverance and supplication for all saints. Vs.19: and for me, that utterance may be given unto me that I may open my mouth boldly to make known the mystery of the gospel.

Praying always with all Prayer and supplication in the Spirit and watching thereunto with all perseverance and supplication for all saints.

We cannot spend all our time on our knees we can have a prayerful attitude at all times, you do not have to pray a long prayer just have Faith in Jesus, there are times I walk around just calling out his name JESUS. There is power in that name. We do not have to walk around like we made heaven and earth like we own everything. Paul said to pray without ceasing, means to abide in the presence of the Father. Having a continual cry from the heart for His Grace and blessing. Paul wrote powerful letters of encouragement from prison.

Vs. 18 Paul was not asking the Ephesians to pray that his chains would be removed but that he would continue to speak boldly for Christ in spite of them God can use us in any circumstance to do his will, even as we pray for a change in our times we should also pray that God will accomplish his plan through us right where we are. While Jesus was here in the flesh, he often prayed to the Father now if Jesus prayed, what about you and me.

Prayer is a conversation of the heart with God, there is no peace without the Grace of God. There is no grace of God without Prayer. Prayer is what we do when we are done struggling with a problem and are ready to call forth its solution. Prayer is about allowing God to do something through you: Amen

Somebody is thinking I pray, and I pray, but seem like I can't get an answer, does God answer all Prayers? He said if you abide in me, and my words abide in you, you will ask what you desire and it shall be done for you.

Meet these requirements and your prayers will be answered; the answer is sometimes immediately, and sometimes the answer is delayed. Martha and Mary's prayers were delayed, and sometimes, the answer is NO. When God answers with a NO, He always accompanies the answer with peace and Grace. God answers all our prayers not according to our wishes but according to His perfect will.

This reminds me of a prayer meeting that was going on at

Sister Mary house, the Bible tells us that Peter was kept in prison, but constant Prayer was offered up to God by the saints of God. There is power in Prayer, we don't have time to pray until we want the Lord to do something for us, then we'll find the time we'll make all kinds of promises. Lord if you heal my body this time I'll do better and time we feel better we forget about what we promise the Lord.

Throughout the Bible, God's people are commanded to pray at all times, we are to pray in all seasons. In sickness or depression, sadness, or grief. No matter what our situation might be, we're to pray without ceasing, we are to pray without ceasing in everything give thanks.

Thank God for the many blessing He sends our way as well as for the trials which He allows us to face to mold us in Christ image. We pray because there is joy in Prayer; there is power in Prayer.

Some people will say I pray but seen like I just can't get a pray through to Jesus. The word of God tells us if you abide in me, and my words abide in you, He Urge us not to cease praying when we do not see our problems disappear immediately, we will stop praying, Oh litter faith. Some people who wait until they are in trouble then they pray. Sometimes instead of asking him for more things, we need to thank and praise Him for what He already has done for us.

Waiting on God is not easy often, it seems that he isn't answering our prayers, or we think he doesn't understand how urgent our situation is. The God that I serve is worth waiting for through our waiting he is teaching us.

Prayer can release our tensions in times of emotional stress; many people don't pray; because they think that they can fix the problems. As long as you think you can fix the problem, God will not here you. There was a certain slave girl possessed, she was a fortune telling. This girl followed Paul and Silas and cried out, saying these men are the servants of the highest God who proclaim to us the way of salvation.

She did this for many days, it also tells us that Paul turned and said to that Spirit, I command you in the name of Jesus Christ to come out of her. When her master saw that their hope of profit was gone. They take Paul and Silas brought of them to the magistrate and told them these men being Jews are trouble in our city.

They tore off their clothes and commanded them to be beaten with rods, and then put them into prison, they didn't put them into just any cell, they were put into an inner cell. That means it was probably dark, cold, and uncomfortable with no way to escape.

Their backs were hurting and bleeding from the beaten. Naturally speaking, they probably didn't feel much like praising the Lord. They had committed no crime, they were put in the most dangerous prison. They didn't give up on God no matter what our circumstances may be just holding on. They forgot about being hurt because at midnight, they were praising the Lord.

Midnight is a dark time in our lives, but these two men of God were not murmuring, complaining, or grumbling. We need to learn how to praise the Lord in the midnight hour. Midnight is going to come in all our lives, and when it happens, we don't have no control over it. We can praise our way out, praise releases God's power, Paul and Silas didn't complain, they put their trust in God. In their midnight hour, they prayed until circumstances was change. There is something about a midnight prayer. Prayer is our commutation with God.

Paul and Silas were beaten put in jail, they could have asked why we didn't do anything wrong. They could have been feeling sorry for themselves. I believe while they were in prison, they had prayer meetings going on at mother Mary house. I think they had a church in prison. In my mind, Paul said I will sing a song, What a friend we have in Jesus, and Silas prayed a prayer. Lord, we didn't do anything wrong, but we are down here in jail, and Lord, we can't do anything until you come. We are down in the coldest part of the prison, lockdown but we know that you are in charge.

The Bible says that another caretaker was listening, if it had not been for Prayer and Faith, somebody would have lost there mind. Suddenly there was a great earthquake, the foundations of the prison were shaken. The prison real and rock and immediately all the doors were opened. The caretaker of the prison awaking out of his sleep, seeing the prison door open. He drew out his sword to kill himself, he thought the prisoner had fled. Paul told him to do yourself no harm we are all here. There is something about prayer changes thing.

Have you ever felt that God didn't hear your prayers? Be sure you are praying with a willing spirit. Be ready to do what God wants, God responds to his obedient children. Prayer is our approach to God, and we are to come boldly unto the throne of Grace.

Now we can have eternal life through Faith in Him, How? Because he broke the power of death with his resurrection. We do not deserve to be saved, but God offers us salvation anyway all we have to do is believe and accept his offer. When God forgives our sins, our record is wiped clean.

CHAPTER 16

The Power Twins

The power of Patience is a working power, sometimes Faith has a tendency to waver, but Patience always comes to Faith's aid to make it stand. Faith and Patience are the power twins.

Faith is the substance of the things we hope for, Patience without Faith has no content. Some people believe that trials and tribulations develop Faith, trials and tribulations do not develop Faith.

Faith cometh by hearing, and hearing by the word of God. Trial and tribulations develop Patience (Romans 5:3) Paul says we glory in tribulation also knowing that tribulation worketh patience. Paul says glory in your tribulation means rejoicing in suffering. How do we rejoice when there is a pain in the body? Faith helps us, trails develop our Patience, it strengthens us and gives us a deeper trust in God.

The Bible did not say if we face trials, but when we meet them if we have not been through anything just wait a while. (James 1:4) God desires to make us complete (perfect) He is not going to keep us from pain. Pain helps us to be complete, instead of complaining about our struggles, we should see them as an opportunity for growth. I thank God for promising to be with us in our rough times we ask him to help us solve our problems or give us the strength to endure them.

Then be patient God will not leave us alone with our problems He is right by our side, James wants believers not only to hear the word but put it into action make sure your Faith is more than just a statement.

The Bible said that Faith is the substance of thing hoped for, the evidence of things not seen. Faith enables our soul to treat the future as present and the invisible as seen. Confidence is knowing before seeing, Faith knows we are healed before we are healed. Faith knows that Jesus is coming back for his church before he comes.

(Philippian 4:19) That he will supply all our needs according to his riches in glory by Christ Jesus, Whatever we need on the earth, he will always provide it. Anyone who draws back anyone looks back anyone put their hands to the plow and looks back from Christ and deliberately keeps on sinning, God shall have no pleasure in him or her, they will face eternal damnation.

Fear is not a mental force, fear is a spiritual force, God created a man called Adam and God gave this man Faith Adam was called the Son of God because he was born of God, then he breathed into him the breath of life. God's Spirit was breathed into Adam, with the Faith he had dominion over the forces of nature everything that walked, crawled, everything in the sea. He had the authority to name everything. He had the power to rule the earth. Adam gave the authority that God give him into the hands of Satan.

The faith force that was born into Adam when God breathed His life into him was perverted and turned into the power that we know and recognize as FEAR. Fear ruled Adam from that moment when God inner the cool of the day. The first words from Adam's mouth were I was afraid. They tell us about a gift of God's Faith that was given to you to keep it to yourself. God made both man and woman in his image. Neither man nor woman is made more in the image of God than the other. From the beginning, the Bible places both men and women at the pinnacle of creation, neither sex is elevated, and neither is depreciated.

The Bible is talking about a gift of God's Faith that was given to you to keep – It Is Yours. The just shall live by Faith, Noah lived by Faith he did all God commanded. Job lived by Faith he was tested beyond imagination.

Ruth lived by Faith left what she had for something far more greater. Easter lived by Faith if I perish let me perish. Phillip lived by Faith he was a man lived by the Spirit. Enoch lives by Faith was translated that he should not see death. Priscilla lived by Faith; she was a pillar of the early church. By Faith, Mary Magdalene stayed at the graves of Jesus all night long. By Faith, we understand how the world was from. By Faith Shadrach, Meshach, and Abed-Nego walked out of a fiery furnace, by Faith Daniels walked out the lion Den by Faith, Paul and Saul walked out of prison at mil -night, By Faith Jesus got up from a borrowed tomb, by Faith we got up this morning made it to church, by Faith we will make it back home.

Trust in the Lord with all your heart lean not on your own understanding, By Faith, we know that Jesus is coming back stand on your Faith. Faith is a powerful force, it will change things Faith will change your heart Faith will change circumstances, Faith will move mountains.

The voice of patients says I know God's Word is right I will not be moved by what I see or what I feel I will only be driven by the Word of God I will wait patiently and rest on the Lord. Job did not understand why he was suffering; he was a man of Faith, Patience, generous, and very caring, very wealthy. Life is brief and full of trouble Job said I'm going to be Patience and keep the Faith.

At times believers may actually suffer more than unbelievers because those who follow God may become Satan's individual targets. Believers, therefore, may have to endure hardship, persecution, or testing. This was the case with Job. We must be prepared for Satan's attacks. When we suffer, we must not conclude that God had abandoned us (he did not leave Job). Consistent Faith is the way to defeat Satan.

In his grief, Job wanted to give in, to be freed from his discomfort, and to die. But God did not grant Job's request. He had a higher plan for him. Our tendency, like Job's, is to want to give up and get out when the going gets rough. To trust God in the good times is commendable, but to trust him during the difficult times test us to our limits and exercises our Faith. In your struggles, large or small, believe that God is in control. In his mercy and Grace, he will take care of you.

CHAPTER 17

The Lamb of God

(R evelation 1:9) I John who also is your brother and companion in the tribulation and in the Kingdom and Patience of Jesus Christ was in the Isle that is called Patmos for the word of God, and for the testimony of Jesus Christ. Vs. 10 I was in the Spirit on the Lord's day and heard behind me a great voice as of a trumpet.

Let us look at this passage today. I believe that the one thing that holds our attention in this Revelation is that John couldn't open the book. In this scripture, it is really challenging us. It is really challenging us to rise to a new level another level so that we will be able to see what his power is all about. We will be able to know what the further holds.

(Revelation 1:7) John is announcing the return of Jesus to earth 'Second coming will be visible and victorious. All the people will see him arrive. And they will know it is. When he comes, the conquer evil Judge all people according to their deeds.

"They also which pierced him" could refer to the Roman soldiers who pierced Jesus' soldiers hung on them as he hung on the cross or to the Jews who were responsible for his death. John saw this event with his own eyes, and he never forgot the horror of it.,

Alpha and Omega are the first and the last letters of the Greek alphabet. The Lord God is the beginning and the end. God the Father is the enteral Lord and Ruler of the past, past. Present, and future. Without him, you have nothing eternal, nothing that can change your life, nothing that can save from sin. Is that the Lord your reason for living, the Alpha and Omega" or your life? Honor the One who is the beginning and the end of all existence. Wisdom and power.

This man like unto the Son of man" is Jesus himself the title "Son of man" occurs many times in the Bible. Blessed is he that readeth and they that hear the words of this Prophecy and keep those things which are written therein for the time is at hand. Satan would love to rob us of the special blessing God he promised to those who will read and hear the Words of this book. Vs. 7 Behold he cometh with clouds and every eye shall see him, and they also which pierced him, and all kindreds of the earth shall wail because of him even so, Amen

John is announcing the return of Jesus to earth. Jesus second coming will be visible and victorious all people will see him arrive; everybody will know it is Jesus.

John tells us in (Revelation 20:11-15) This is a reference we will talk about this again and I saw a great white throne, and him that sat on it from whose face the east and the heaven fled away.

And there was found no place for them, and I saw the dead, Small and significant stand before God, and the books were opened, and another book was open, which is the book of life. And the dead were judged out of those things which were written in the books, according to their works.

And the sea gave up the dead which was in it and death and Hell delivered up the body which was in them. And they were judged every man according to their works. And death and Hell were cast into the lake of fire.

Jesus knocked at the door of our hearts, but people are so busy enjoying a worldly pleasure that they do not notice that Jesus is trying to enter. The joys of this world can be dangerous, letting Jesus in your heart is your only hope for everlasting life. He is knocking he is patiently trying to get through to us.

He is not going to break and enter, but He is knocking there is power all power on the other side of that door. Jesus said I'm standing at the door. I am knocking on every sinner's heart. If you don't know me to open up to let me in time is getting short.

Jesus said for us to watch, for ye know not what hour your Lord doth come. He could come before night or morning will you be ready. I'm going to wait until things in the world get better, the conditions will become worse and worse and then suddenly the Lord will come.

God offers salvation to all people many people put off a decision for Christ, thinking that there will be a better time. They could easily miss their opportunity altogether. There is no time like the present to receive God's forgiveness. Don't let anything hold you back from coming to Christ, the right time is now. The scripture tells us that there is one door into heaven, Jesus said I am the door if any man enters in he shall be saved. If you have not let Jesus in your life into your heart. Open your door, let Him come in.

John said I was in the Spirit on the Lord's day and heard behind me a great voice as a trumpet saying I am Alpha and Omega the first and the last. Jesus said to John, write this in a book and send it to the seven Churches.

Which are in Asia, unto Ephesus, unto Smyrna and unto Pergamos unto Thyatira, Sardis and unto Philadephia and unto Laodicea. John said I turned to see who was talking to me, and I saw seven golden Candlesticks, and in the seven Candlesticks, one like unto the Son of man. Clothed with a garment down to the feet and girded about the chest with a golden band. His head and his hair were white like wool as white as snow, and his eyes were as a flame of fire. His feet like unto fine brass as if they burned in a furnace and his voice as the sound of many drinks of water.

No matter what the churches face, Jesus protects them with

his love and power, he is still here today through his Holy Spirit. John recognized Jesus because he lived with him has heard Jesus preach many sermons, and as the glorified Son of God at the transfiguration. This man like unto the Son of man is Jesus himself. His white hair indicates his wisdom and divine nature.

Daniel 7:9 He saw Jesus His white garment was white as snow, and his hair of his head like pure wool. Nebuchadnezzar saw him in the furnace. His bright eyes symbolize judgment of all evil. The golden band across his chest reveals him as the high priest who goes into God's presence to obtain forgiveness of sin for those who have believed in him.

There is probably not a book in the entire Bible, which is less read and understood that the text of Revelation. Not only is the book call Revelation to encourage us to read it, but it is the only book in the Bible in which God promises a special blessing to those who will read and study it.

John was the only Apostle to die a natural death he was exiled on this Isle called Patmos while writing the Revelation and was later released at the time he wrote his three other epistles. We do not know how old John was, but he outlives all the apostles, including Paul. For by Grace, we have been saved through Faith, and that not of ourselves it is the gift of God.

Even Faith is not of our self it to is the gift of God. Paul tells us that Faith comes by hearing and hearing by the word of God. Without Faith, there is no salvation. Our sins may be, and many but God grace is more excellent. Christ settled the question of crime on the cross when he cried it is finished.

When we accepted Jesus as Lord and Savior now we are born again children of God. The world does not know us why? Because the world does not know Jesus, God paid dearly with the life of his Son Jesus Christ.

He paid the highest price he could pay, Jesus accepted our punishment. He paid the price for our sins. Then he offered us the new life he had brought for us. Amen

I am so glad we don't have to walk this road by ourselves, God sent Jesus Christ to die for us. Not because we were good enough, because He loved us so much. Whenever you feel uncertain about God's love for you, remember that he loved you even before you turned to Him.

Sometimes instead of asking Jesus for more things, we need to thank and praise Him for what He already has done for us. Leave the door of your heart open to God, let him in don't get upset about little things. The conditions of the church should not alarm and confuse us, this evidence of the coming again of the Head of the Church the Lord Jesus.

Revelation Chapter 3 ends with a closed door that Jesus stands and knocks. Revelation Chapter 4 begins with an open door through which Jesus will return.

Revelation 3:20 Behold I stand at the door and knot if any man hears my voice and opens the door I will come into him and will eat with him and he with me. He does not do-breaking and entering, but he is knocking, he allows us to decide whether or not to open our lives to Him.

(John 4:10-15) Jesus answered and said unto her, If thou knew the gift of God, and who it is that saith to thee, Give me to drink; thou would have asked of him, and he would have given thee living water.

What did Jesus mean by "living water"? As our bodies hunger and thirst, so do our souls. But our souls need spiritual food and water. The woman confused the two kinds of water, perhaps because no one had ever talked with her about her spiritual hunger and thirst before. We would not think of depriving our bodies of food and water when they hunger for the theist. Why then should we deny our souls? The living Word, Jesus Christ, and his Word the Bible can satisfy our hungry and thirsty souls.

The woman mistakenly believed that if she received the water Jesus offered, she would not have to return to the well each day. She was interested in Jesus' message because she thought it could make her life more comfortable. But if that were always the case, people would accept Christ's message for the wrong reasons. Christ did not come to take away challenges, but to change us on the inside and to empower us to deal with problems from God's perspective.

(Revelation 22:17) And the Spirit and the bride say, Come. And let him that heareth say, Come. And let him that is athirst come. And whosoever will let him take the water of life freely.

When Jesus met the Samaritan woman at the well, he told her of the living water that he could supply. This image is used again as Christ invites anyone to come and drink of the water of life. He is inviting all people everywhere to come. Salvation cannot be earned, but God gives it freely. We live in a world desperately thirsty for living water, and many are dying of thirst. But it is still not too late. Let us invite everyone to come and drink.

We don't know the day or the hour, but Jesus is coming soon and unexpectedly. This is good news to those who trust him, but a terrible message for those who have rejected him and stand under judgment. Early means "at any moment," and we must be ready for him, always prepared for his return. Would Jesus' sudden appearance catch you off guard? AMEN

CHAPTER 18

There is Power In Prayer

Prayer is a conversation of the heart with God, through Prayer, we align ourselves with our Creator, and his presence is revealed to us. We grow in our love and worship of Him. Also, when we are united with our Lord through Prayer, our life becomes fuller, more productive, more joyous, and more peaceful.

Prayer is a cleansing process, washing our thoughts, feelings, motives, and will purifying the entire being including the heart, thus enabling us to see God, for without purity no one can see God.

A good prayer life, in my estimation, is being aware of God's presence and being transparent with Him about what I am experiencing, sometimes involves a formal audible prayer, but more often it is a thought life that is shared with God."

Prayer is fed by Faith, Jesus prayed with unwavering Faith to His heavenly Father, a faith that lasted until His death. He taught us to pray also with childlike Faith in God, believing that the One who loves us hears our prayers. We can not be fearful and praying to God; we must have Faith knowing that God is going to answer your Prayer.

Prayer should be steady and persevering as His Prayer was even when no answer comes or when no relief is in sight. "Watch and Pray," He says, "Seek and knock," until the door that reveals God's Holy will be opened.

Prayer is a cleansing process, washing our thoughts, feelings, motives, and will, purifying the entire being including the heart, thus enabling us to see God, for without purity no one can see God. Prayer is what you do when you are done struggling with a problem, and you are to call forth its solution. Prayer is not about trying to get God to do something to you or give something to you. It is about allowing God to do something through you.

Having a spirited prayer is one of the most important things in your walk with Christ. We Christians learn to pray through Jesus Christ, who not only teaches us to pray but also prayed himself. His Prayer filled the Gospel Did Jesus himself have to learn to pray? Yes, he did True He was the Son of God who knew all things; nevertheless, as one like us, he had to learn to pray while growing up. In the village of Nazareth, Mary and Joseph guided his first steps in Prayer at home in the synagogue at Nazareth, in the temple of Jerusalem, he learned the rhythms and words of Jewish Prayer.

Jesus prayed to God with a distinct intimacy. God was his Father, and He was God Son there was a childlike, filial quality to his Prayer Jesus prayed regularly, His first disciples recalled, He prayed before decisive moments beginning with His baptism and as he faces his passion and death. He prayed in times of human weakness and death, as he did at the grave of Lazarus. He frequently prayed to give thanks. Prayer was steady and confident that God's will was for his good.

What can we learn from the Prayer of Jesus? First, a sincere Prayer should come from the heart. He prayed from within not just words or gestures His Prayer was not based only on feeling or passing emotions. Prayer comes from within, beyond a level of feelings from us. "Go into the inner room, "Jesus says," and there pray to your Father who hears you." Sometimes Prayer from the heart from the "inner room" takes the form of words, at other times, it may be like his wordless cry.

Secondly, Prayer is fed by FAITH. Jesus prayed with unwavering Faith to his Heavenly Father, a father a faith that lasted until his death He taught us to pray also with childlike Faith in God, believing that the One who loves us hears our prayers.

Prayer is an attitude it involves more than just making requests, Prayer is communicating with God. You can live in a manner of Prayer, always being communion and fellowship with your heavenly Father every hour of the day. To get results in Prayer, you must be convinced one first face God wants to answer your prayers. In fact, he is as ready and willing to answer you as He was to answer Jesus during His early ministry. This may be difficult for you to believe, but it is true.

To understand what Prayer is, it helps you to realize what it is not. Prayer is not an emotional release; it is not an escape valve. It is much more than just asking God for a favor, perhaps most important of all Prayer is not a religious exercise.

You should be praying for results every time you pray, do not just speak empty words, Jesus said in (Matthew 6:7) "But when ye pray, use not vain repetitions, as the heathen do: for they think that they shall be heard for their much speaking."

The beauty of your Prayer does not get the ear of God, He responds to FAITH, to explain, let me give you an example from my own experience. Not long after I became a Christian, I asked a minister to pray for me. I was expecting to hear a long, long beautiful prayer one that would cause people to fall on their knees in repentance before God. The key to success in Prayer is expecting results many Christians think I will pray and maybe something will happen, they say, "I'm just hoping and praying." If you are hoping to get results, you will never receive from God. "Hoping to get" is not the same as "believing you receive." The promises of God bring you to hope in hopeless situations. However, hope has no substance in itself, I hope to get healed someday." You desire to receive it anytime? But sometimes never come, Faith brings hope into reality and gives substance to it. Hebrews 11:1 says. "Now, faith is the substance of things hoped for, the evidence of things not seen." The object of hope becomes a reality through Faith, hope is always in the future. Faith is still now.

We know God answers prayers, but there are times we want Him to answer on our time and not His. When we're impatient, we lose Faith that He will answer our Prayer, so we try to take matters into our hands. We try to control our lives, we need to have Faith that He will provide for us because He loves us. God answers all our prayers, not according to our wishes, but according to His Perfect will. Amen!